MOSAIK 2

German Language and Culture

Student Activities Manual

VISTA®
HIGHER LEARNING

ISBN: 978-1-68005-095-0

3 4 5 6 7 8 9 PP 21 20 19 18 17

Table of Contents

Introduction

The **MOSAIK 2** Workbook

Completely coordinated with the **MOSAIK 2** textbook, the Workbook for **MOSAIK 2** provides additional practice of the vocabulary and grammar presented in each of the textbook's four chapters. The Workbook will also help you build your reading and writing skills in German. Icons and page references in the **Ressourcen** boxes of the **MOSAIK 2** textbook correlate the Workbook to your textbook, letting you know where you can find additional practice for a given vocabulary set or grammar point. Answers to the Workbook activities are located in a separate Answer Key for teachers.

Each lesson's Workbook activities focus on developing your reading and writing skills as they reinforce the vocabulary and grammar of the corresponding textbook lesson and chapter. Activity formats include, but are not limited to: true/false, multiple choice, fill-in-the-blanks, sentence completion, sentence expansion, and answering questions. You will also find activities based on maps, photographs, and illustrations.

Reflecting the organization of the textbook, each Workbook chapter contains two lessons, each of which features **Kontext** and **Strukturen** sections.

The **MOSAIK 2** Lab Manual

Completely coordinated with the **MOSAIK 2** textbook, the Lab Manual for **MOSAIK 2** provides additional practice of the vocabulary and grammar presented in each of the textbook's four chapters. The Lab Manual will also help you build your listening and speaking skills in German. Icons and page references in the **Ressourcen** boxes of the **MOSAIK 2** textbook correlate the Lab Manual to your textbook, letting you know when additional practice is available. Answers to the Lab Manual activities are located in a separate Answer Key for teachers.

The laboratory activities are designed for use with the **MOSAIK 2** Lab Program MP3s on the **MOSAIK 2** Supersite. They focus on building your listening comprehension, speaking, and pronunciation skills in German as they reinforce the vocabulary and grammar of each textbook lesson. The Lab Manual guides you through the Lab MP3 files, providing the printed cues—direction lines, models, charts, drawings, etc.—you will need in order to follow along. You will hear statements, questions, mini-dialogues, conversations, monologues, and many other kinds of listening passages, all recorded by native German speakers. You will encounter a wide range of activities, such as listening-and-repeating exercises, listening-and-speaking practice, listening-and-writing activities, illustration-based activities, and dictations.

Each Lab Manual lesson contains a **Kontext** section that practices the active vocabulary taught in the corresponding textbook lesson. The **Aussprache und Rechtschreibung** section parallels the one found in your textbook, and, in addition, offers a dictation activity. Each laboratory lesson includes sections for each **Strukturen** section presented in the textbook.

The **MOSAIK 2** Video Manual

Each **MOSAIK 2 Fotoroman** episode tells the continuing story of four college students studying in Germany. The video, shot in a variety of locations in Berlin, tells their story. The video modules contain two distinct elements. First, you will see a dramatic episode that brings the themes, vocabulary, grammar, and language functions of the corresponding textbook lesson to life. These episodes are expanded versions of the ones featured in the **Fotoroman** sections of your textbook. Each episode ends with a **Zusammenfassung** segment in which a narrator calls out key language from the video, highlighting functional vocabulary and grammatical structures used by the characters.

The video activities will guide you through the video modules, providing activities that check your comprehension while also giving you the opportunity to offer your own opinions and describe your own experiences.

We hope that you will find the **MOSAIK 2** Student Activities Manual to be a useful language learning resource and that it will help you to increase your German language skills in a productive, enjoyable way.

The **MOSAIK 2** *authors and Vista Higher Learning editorial staff*

Kapitel 1

Lektion 1A

KONTEXT

1 **Was ist richtig?** Choose the word that best completes each sentence.

1. Andrea gibt Hans einen _____ zum Geburtstag.
   a. Abschluss   b. Jahrestag   c. Kuss

2. Der _____ gibt eine Party.
   a. Gast   b. Gastgeber   c. Architekt

3. Die Gäste _____ bis spät in die Nacht.
   a. feiern   b. bekommen   c. schenken

4. Ritas _____ ist ein Rucksack.
   a. Ballon   b. Geschenk   c. Freundschaft

5. Die _____ sind seit vier Stunden verheiratet.
   a. Gastgeber   b. Gäste   c. Frischvermählten

6. Die Familie _____ viele Gäste zum Silvesterabend _____.
   a. stößt ... an   b. lädt ... ein   c. kauft ... ein

2 **Assoziationen** Match each description with the corresponding event.

Beschreibung

1. _____ Das Baby ist eine Stunde alt.

2. _____ Die Großeltern sind 45 Jahre verheiratet.

3. _____ Nach 40 Jahren arbeitet Frau Schwarz nicht mehr (*no longer*).

4. _____ Mia bekommt Ballons und ein Geschenk.

5. _____ Um Mitternacht gibt Matthias seiner Frau einen Kuss.

6. _____ Die Familie feiert am 25. und 26. Dezember.

Anlass

a. der Geburtstag

b. Weihnachten

c. Silvester

d. der Jahrestag

e. in Rente gehen

f. die Geburt

3 **Wir feiern** Complete each sentence with a word from the list.

bekommen	in Rente gehen
einladen	den Abschluss machen
keinen Spaß haben	überraschen

1. Der Gastgeber _____ seine Freunde _____.

2. „Die Party _____ mich sehr", sagt Hanna an ihrem Geburtstag.

3. Opa ist jetzt 65 und er _____.

4. Onkel Philip _____ an der Party _____. Er ist müde und will schlafen.

5. Johanna _____ an der Universität Mainz _____.

6. Der junge Mann _____ viele Geschenke zum Geburtstag.

Workbook

4 **Fragen** Answer the questions about yourself using complete sentences.

1. Wann haben Sie Geburtstag?

_____

2. Feiern Sie am 24. oder 25. Dezember Weihnachten?

_____

3. An welchem Tag feiern Ihre Eltern den Jahrestag ihrer Hochzeit?

_____

4. Wer gibt am Wochenende eine Party?

_____

5. Wie feiern Sie Silvester?

_____

6. Mögen Sie Kuchen und Torten?

_____

5 **Beschreiben Sie** Describe the pictures using complete sentences. Be creative.

1.    2.    3.    4.

1. _____

_____

_____

2. _____

_____

_____

3. _____

_____

_____

4. _____

_____

_____

STRUKTUREN

1A.1 The *Perfekt* (Part 1)

1 **Infinitiv** Write the infinitive form of each past participle.

1. Wir haben Vater mit einem schönen Geschenk überrascht. _____

2. Haben Sie die Professorin eingeladen, Frau Neumann? _____

3. Ich habe viel Torte gegessen. _____

4. Ihr habt Apfelsaft getrunken. _____

5. Schön! Du hast dem Baby drei Ballons gebracht. _____

6. Es hat leider am Silvesterabend geregnet. _____

2 **Was fehlt?** Complete the sentences with the **Perfekt** forms of the verbs provided.

1. Ich _____ die Sängerin gern _____. (hören)

2. Du _____ der Gastgeberin _____. (helfen)

3. Wir _____ unseren Freunden eine Karte _____. (schreiben)

4. Anna _____ an Fabians Kuss _____. (denken)

5. Ihr _____ Alex mit Ballons und Geschenken _____. (gratulieren)

6. Lukas und Katharina _____ ein neues Haus _____. (finden)

3 **Bilden Sie Sätze** Create six logical sentences in the **Perfekt** with one element from each column.

A	B	C
du	seinen Hund Simon	arbeiten
Herr Müller	mit deiner Cousine	lernen
ich	an meinem Geburtstag	nennen
ihr	unsere Freunde in der Stadt	öffnen
Lina und Tim	die Hochzeitskarte	sprechen
wir	für die Deutschprüfung	treffen

1. _____

2. _____

3. _____

4. _____

5. _____

6. _____

4 **Eine E-Mail** Complete the email with the correct **Perfekt** forms of the words in the list.

essen	haben	schlafen
feiern	öffnen	schreiben
geben	schenken	tanzen

Von: lina.martin@deutsche-mail.de
An: margretchen@brdpost.de
Datum: 8. September

Liebe Margret,

hallo, wie geht's? Du (1) _____ mir so eine nette Geburtstagskarte _____!
Vielen Dank!! Ich (2) _____ sie an meinem Geburtstag _____. Meine
Freunde (3) _____ eine Party für mich _____. Wir (4) _____ bei
Christian _____. Wir (5) _____ zu guter Musik _____.
Später (6) _____ wir einen leckeren Kuchen _____. Wir
(7) _____ viel Spaß _____. Am nächsten Morgen (8) _____ ich
lange _____. Eine schöne Party.

Bis bald!

Lina

P.S. Meine Tante (9) _____ mir ein Essen in einem feinen Restaurant _____.

5 **Beschreiben Sie** Write a sentence in the **Perfekt** for each picture using the words provided.

Beispiel

kein Glück in der Liebe haben
Klara
Klara hat kein Glück in der Liebe gehabt.

Klara

ein Geschenk bringen	ihre Hochzeit feiern
einen Literaturabschluss machen	Kuchen und Torten kaufen

1. Ben, Emma   2. Julius   3. die Frischvermählten   4. Anna

1. _____

2. _____

3. _____

4. _____

1A.2 Accusative pronouns

1 **Verbinden Sie** Match each question with a likely response.

1. _____ Hast du Jutta zur Hochzeit eingeladen?
2. _____ Wo soll ich das Fleisch kaufen?
3. _____ Wohin müssen die Freunde die Karten schicken?
4. _____ Ist die Party für mich?
5. _____ Wer ruft den Gastgeber an?
6. _____ Geht Ali ohne uns auf die Party?

a. Sie müssen sie nach Düsseldorf schicken.
b. Viele Gäste rufen ihn an.
c. Ja, er geht ohne euch.
d. Ja, ich habe sie eingeladen.
e. Ja, sie ist für dich.
f. Du sollst es bei Schröder kaufen.

2 **Eine Einladung** Complete the conversation with the pronouns in the list. You may use some words more than once.

dich	euch	mich
es	ihn	sie

MATTHIAS Wie heißt du? Ich kenne (1) _____.

ANITA Ich heiße Anita. Du kennst _____?

MATTHIAS Ja. Ich heiße Matthias. Ich habe (3) _____ und meinen Freund Holger in der Bibliothek getroffen. Ich kenne (4) _____ von der Filmvorlesung.

ANITA Ja, wir haben eine Prüfung gehabt. (5) _____ war (*was*) am Mittwoch und wir haben am Dienstag in der Bibliothek Mathe gelernt.

MATTHIAS Holger hat von der Dozentin gesprochen. Er findet (6) _____ sehr gut.

ANITA Er hat recht. Ohne (7) _____ ist Mathematik langweilig.

MATTHIAS Dann habe ich (8) _____ auch in der Mensa gesehen.

ANITA Wirklich? Ich finde das Essen da nicht so gut. Wie findest du (9) _____?

MATTHIAS Nicht sehr gut. Wo isst du gern?

ANITA Zu Hause. Ich gehe auch mit Freunden zum Italiener. Isst du auch gern da?

MATTHIAS Ja, sehr gern.

ANITA Gut. Das nächste Mal (*next time*) rufe ich (10) _____ an.

3 **Minidialoge** Restate the second line of each dialogue with an accusative pronoun.

1. —Wen siehst du da?
   —Ich sehe meinen Freund!
   —Ich sehe _____!

2. —Was sucht sie?
   —Sie sucht ihr Buch über Deutschland.
   —Sie sucht _____.

3. —Wen ladet ihr ein?
   —Wir laden unsere große Familie ein.
   —Wir laden _____ ein.

4. —Wen fragt sie?
   —Sie fragt mich und meine sieben Geschwister.
   —Sie fragt _____.

5. —Für wen kaufen die Kinder Geschenke?
   —Die Kinder kaufen Geschenke für mich und meine Frau.
   —Sie kaufen sie für _____.

6. —Wen brauchst du, mein Kind?
   —Ich brauche meine Mutti! Ich brauche
   _____, Mutti!

4 **Aussagen** Make a statement about each object and substitute a pronoun for the object.

> **Beispiel**
> ohne den Rucksack / meine Bücher nicht tragen
> *Ohne ihn kann ich meine Bücher nicht tragen.*

1. das Eis / bestellen

2. das Mineralwasser / kalt trinken

3. die Birnen / auf dem Markt kaufen

4. ohne den Kuli / nicht schreiben

5. ohne das Fahrrad / nicht zur Schule fahren

6. die Tomate / nicht ohne Salz essen

1. _____
2. _____
3. _____
4. _____
5. _____
6. _____

5 **Die Großmutter** Your grandmother is talking about her life. Ask follow-up questions for her statements. Use pronouns for the direct objects.

> **Beispiel**
> 1955 habe ich Konrad Adenauer kennen gelernt.
> *Wo hast du ihn kennen gelernt?*

1. 1960 habe ich die Beatles gehört.

_____

2. 1965 habe ich Marlene Dietrich gesehen.

_____

3. 1970 habe ich die ersten Artischocken gegessen.

_____

4. 1985 habe ich „Kassandra" von Christa Wolf gelesen.

_____

5. 1990 habe ich ein Buch geschrieben.

_____

1A.3 Dative pronouns

1 **Dativpronomen erkennen** Identify the dative pronoun in each sentence.

1. Die Gäste geben ihm ein Geschenk. _____
2. Ich gratuliere euch zur Hochzeit. _____
3. Sie bringen ihr die Hausaufgaben. _____
4. Der Gastgeber dankt ihnen. _____
5. Kann ich Ihnen helfen, Herr Neumann? _____
6. Mir gefällt der Film nicht. _____
7. Der kleine Hund folgt dir in den Garten. _____
8. Mutti, kaufst du uns bitte einen neuen Ball? _____

2 **Dativpronomen** Substitute a dative pronoun for each word in parentheses.

1. Wir öffnen _____ die Tür. (dem Hund)
2. Der kleine Willi gibt _____ einen Kuss. (seiner Mutter)
3. Die Gastgeberin gibt _____ Ballons. (den Gästen)
4. Wie gefällt _____ diese Hochzeitsfeier? (Mia und Maria)
5. Papa muss _____ ein Schulbuch kaufen. (meinem kleinen Bruder)
6. Warum antwortet er _____ nicht? (du)
7. Was macht Hanna mit _____? (den Geschenken)
8. Die kleine Katze will _____ in das Feinkostgeschäft folgen. (Frau Wagner)

3 **Nominativ, Akkusativ, Dativ** Answer the questions with pronouns wherever possible.

> **Beispiel**
> Schmeckt der Fisch dem Vater?
> Ja, er schmeckt ihm.

1. Gibt Julia ihrem Bruder den Keks?

_____

2. Schreiben wir unserer Tante?

_____

3. Gratulieren Sie den Frischvermählten?

_____

4. Korrigiert die Professorin dir die Prüfung?

_____

5. Hat die Köchin uns Meeresfrüchte gekocht?

_____

Workbook

4   Bilder beschreiben Write a short description of each picture. Replace the word in parentheses with a dative pronoun.

> **Beispiel**
>
> ich / zeigen / (meinen Eltern) / die schlechten Noten
> *Ich zeige ihnen die schlechten Noten.*

1. Paula / geben / (dem Verkäufer) / das Geld

   _____

2. der Verkäufer / danken / (Paula)

   _____

3. Jasmin / zeigen / (ihren Freunden) / das Fotoalbum

   _____

4. (dem Professor) / gefallen / das Buch

   _____

5   Schreiben Sie Answer the questions using dative pronouns.

> **Beispiel**
>
> Gehst du mit deiner Freundin ins Café, Lukas?
> *Ja, ich gehe mit ihr ins Café.*

1. Gefällt euch das neue Restaurant, Fabian und Erik?

   _____

2. Bringt dir dein Freund das Geschenk, Lara?

   _____

3. Wohnen Ihre Kinder bei Ihnen, Herr Atatürk?

   _____

4. Glaubst du uns, Alexander?

   _____

5. Kauft ihr mir ein neues Fahrrad, Vati und Mutti?

   _____

6. Kann ich dir helfen, Philip?

   _____

Kapitel 1 — Lektion 1B

KONTEXT

1 **Was passt nicht?** Indicate the item in each group that doesn't belong.

1. die Baumwolle, das Leder, der Tisch
2. die Socke, die Brille, die Unterwäsche
3. einfarbig, gestreift, fleißig
4. das Papier, der Handschuh, der Mantel
5. braun, blau, kurzärmlig
6. die Seide, das Sweatshirt, die Jeans

2 **Welche Farbe?** State the color commonly associated with each item.

1. Pfeffer ist _____.
2. Papier ist _____.
3. Schokolade ist _____.
4. Das Gras ist _____.
5. Der Ozean ist _____.
6. Der Apfel ist _____.
7. Die Banane ist _____.

3 **Was trägt sie?** Join the sentences to describe what Johanna wears for each activity.

1.   2.   3.   4.

1. Zum Laufen trägt Johanna _____
2. Zur Arbeit trägt sie _____
3. Im Café trägt sie _____
4. Zum Tanzen trägt sie _____

a. ein Kleid aus Seide und braune Schuhe.
b. eine Hose, eine Bluse und schwarze Stiefel.
c. Jeans und ein T-Shirt.
d. ein Trägerhemd und eine kurze Hose.

4 **Was tragen Sie?** In complete sentences, describe what you might wear on each occasion.

> **Beispiel**
>
> bei der Arbeit:
> Ich trage einen Pullover und einen Rock.

1. zur Universität: _____

   _____

2. am Strand: _____

   _____

3. zum Wandern in den Alpen: _____

   _____

4. zur Party: _____

   _____

5. zum Fußballspiel: _____

   _____

6. zum Konzert: _____

   _____

5 **Einkaufen** Read Alexandra's description of her taste in clothing. Then choose four articles of clothing for her to buy, and explain your choices.

Hallo, ich bin Alexandra. Ich gehe nicht gern an den Strand, aber ich mag den Winter. Ich trage gern elegante Kleidung, besonders gern mag ich Jeans. Ich bezahle nicht gern mehr als €100 für ein Kleidungsstück. Ich mag alle Farben außer Schwarz, Lila und Rosa.

	Farben im Angebot
Handschuhe und Schal €10,50	blau, braun, gelb, grau, grün, lila, orange, rosa, rot, schwarz, weiß
Lederjacke €95,99	
Halskette €220,00	
Skistiefel €65,00	
Jeans €59,99	
Hemd €45,50	
T-Shirt €19,99	

_____

_____

_____

_____

_____

_____

_____

STRUKTUREN

1B.1 The *Perfekt* (Part 2)

1   *Haben* **oder** *sein*? Indicate which verbs take **haben** and which take **sein** in the **Perfekt**.

	haben	sein
1. bleiben	○	○
2. tragen	○	○
3. fahren	○	○
4. essen	○	○
5. fallen	○	○
6. lernen	○	○
7. schreiben	○	○
8. gehen	○	○
9. kommen	○	○
10. feiern	○	○

2   **Was fehlt?** Complete each sentence with the correct form of the **haben** or **sein**.

1. Emma _____ nach der Party nach Hause gegangen.

2. _____ du heute schon deine Hausaufgaben gemacht?

3. Der schwarze Anzug _____ nicht viel gekostet.

4. _____ ihr im Sommer viel gereist?

5. Mein Bruder _____ mir grüne Handschuhe geschenkt.

6. _____ du ohne Brille ins Kino gegangen?

7. Julian _____ gestern eine kleine Katze bekommen.

8. Nein! Ich _____ das gestreifte Kleid nicht gekauft.

3   **Eine Postkarte** Complete Simon's postcard with the correct forms of the **Partizip**.

Lieber Philip!

Meine Schwester und ich sind für zwei Wochen nach Berlin (1) _____ (reisen).
Die Zeit hier ist toll (2) _____ (sein). Letzte Woche haben wir ein Museum
(3) _____ (besuchen). Wir sind lange dort (4) _____ (bleiben).
Besonders schön habe ich die ägyptischen Statuen (5) _____ (finden). Die
Stadt ist sehr schön und interessant (6) _____ (werden). Abends sind wir
natürlich in einen großartigen Club (7) _____ (gehen). Wir haben hier in
Berlin viel Spaß (8) _____ (haben).

Bis bald!

Dein Simon

Kapitel 1 Workbook Activities   **11**

4   **Eine Antwort** Complete Philip's answer to Simon with the correct forms of **haben** and **sein** and the correct **Partizip**.

Lieber Simon!

Gestern (1) _____ ich deine Karte aus Berlin _____ (lesen).
Vielen Dank dafür! Ich hoffe, du (2) _____ viel Spaß _____
(haben). Wie (3) _____ ihr denn nach Berlin _____ (fahren)?
Mit dem Auto? Und wo (4) _____ ihr _____ (schlafen)? Im
Hotel? Bei Freunden? (5) _____ ihr viel _____ (sehen)?

Bis nächste Woche!

Dein Philip

5   **Alles schon passiert** Rewrite these sentences in the **Perfekt**.

> **Beispiel**
>
> Meine Freundin adoptiert zwei Katzen.
> Meine Freundin hat zwei Katzen adoptiert.

1. Der Baum wächst schnell.

   _____

2. Ihr reist zusammen nach Berlin.

   _____

3. David reitet oft am Wochenende.

   _____

4. Lina schläft den ganzen Nachmittag.

   _____

5. Du lernst in der Bibliothek, nicht?

   _____

6. Ich kaufe die tollen Schuhe.

   _____

6   **Letztes Jahr** Write four sentences describing something you did last year. Your sentences should include verbs that take **sein** and verbs that take **haben**.

1. _____

2. _____

3. _____

4. _____

1B.2 *Wissen* and *kennen*

1 ***Wissen* oder *kennen*?** Indicate for each sentence whether **wissen** or **kennen** is appropriate.

1. (Weißt / Kennst) du die Uhrzeit?

2. (Weißt / Kennst) du meine Schwester?

3. Ich (weiß / kenne) Berlin ganz gut.

4. Wir (wissen / kennen) nicht, wie er heißt.

5. Aber er (weiß / kennt) meine Probleme sehr genau.

6. Ich habe im Wörterbuch die Antwort gefunden. Jetzt (weiß / kenne) ich es!

2 **Welches Verb?** Decide whether each context requires **wissen** or **kennen**, and complete the sentence with the correct form of the verb.

1. Ich _____ seinen Namen nicht.

2. Fabian _____ unser Land gut.

3. Michael _____ die Antwort nicht.

4. Yusuf _____ Sara schon seit drei Jahren.

5. Wir _____ die Telefonnummer nicht.

6. _____ du den Gastgeber?

7. _____ ihr die Musik von Beethoven?

8. _____ du schon das neue Videospiel?

3 **Informationen finden** State whether the facts, people, and places belong with **kennen** or **wissen**.

die Adresse von Dilara	Maries Eltern
das Anne Frank Haus in Amsterdam	viel über Mode
ihren Familiennamen nicht	ein gutes chinesisches Restaurant
deine Freundin nicht	die Uhrzeit
die Antwort	Wien gut

Ich kenne...   Ich weiß...

1. _____   1. _____

2. _____   2. _____

3. _____   3. _____

4. _____   4. _____

5. _____   5. _____

Workbook

4 **Was passt zusammen?** Describe what these people know or don't know in complete sentences using **kennen** or **wissen** and the phrases provided. Follow the example.

> **Beispiel**
> viel über Schach
> Pauls Opa
> *Pauls Opa weiß viel über Schach.*

> die Stadt nicht gut   viele gute Rezepte.
> viel über deutsche Rockmusik   eine gute Eisdiele

1. Moritz   2. Maria und Lena   3. Stefan   4. Hanna und Dana

1. _____

2. _____

3. _____

4. _____

5 **Gespräche** Complete each conversation with the appropriate present-tense forms of **wissen** or **kennen**.

KLARA Hallo Jana, wie geht es dir?

JANA Hallo Klara! Gut, und wie geht's dir so?

KLARA Danke, auch gut. Sag mal, (1) _____ du einen guten Friseur?

JANA Ja, ich (2) _____ einen sehr guten Friseur.

KLARA (3) _____ du auch die Adresse?

JANA Ja klar, (4) _____ ich sie: Gutenbergstraße 8.

MAX Hallo Sara, na wie geht's dir heute?

SARA Hi Max! Ganz gut, und dir?

MAX Danke, es geht mir gut. (5) _____ du die neue Studentin Megan?

SARA Ja, ich (6) _____ sie. Warum fragst du?

MAX Ich soll sie anrufen. (7) _____ du ihre Telefonnummer?

SARA Leider (8) _____ ich sie nicht. (9) _____ du ihren Freund Jeffrey? Er (10) _____ die Nummer bestimmt.

MAX Ja, er ist in meinem Englischseminar. Ich frage ihn.

1B.3 Two-way prepositions

Workbook

1   **Was ist richtig?** Choose the correct articles and/or pronouns.

1. Wir wohnen über (einer / eine) Schule.
2. Der warme Mantel hängt an (die / der) Tür.
3. Ich lege das gestreifte Kleid auf (den / dem) Stuhl.
4. Unter (den / dem) Tisch liegt meine Katze.
5. Die Verkäuferin hängt das blaue Kleid zwischen (die / den) Mäntel und die Blusen.
6. Philip trägt immer ein T-Shirt über (sein / seinem) Pullover.
7. Hanna schläft immer mit (ihr / ihrem) Hund.
8. Frau Yilmaz braucht einen Hut und geht in (ein / einem) Geschäft.
9. Die schwarze Katze sitzt gern auf (meine / meiner) weißen Jacke.
10. Bist du am Sonntag in (ein / einem) Konzert gegangen?

2   **Was passt?** Complete each sentence with the correct form of the appropriate verb from the list.

hängen	liegen	sitzen	stellen
legen	setzen	stehen	

Lara (1) _____ die Vase auf den Tisch. Die Vase (2) _____ auf dem Tisch.

Er (3) _____ den Mantel in den Schrank. Der Mantel (4) _____ im Schrank.

Moritz (5) _____ die Katze auf die Couch. Die Katze (6) _____ auf der Couch.

Du (7) _____ den Rock auf den Stuhl. Der Rock (8) _____ auf dem Stuhl.

3   **Kurz gesagt** Replace the two-way prepositions and definite articles with common contractions.

1. Jasmin und Niklas waren gestern _____ (in dem) Konzert. Sie sind mit Freunden

    _____ (in das) Konzert gegangen.

2. Meine Mutter stellt die Tasche _____ (an das) Regal. Die Tasche steht

    _____ (an dem) Regal.

3. Paula legt die Wurst _____ (auf das) Brötchen.

4. _____ (An dem) Sonntag gehen wir _____ (in das) Hardrock-Café.

5. _____ (In dem) Sommer gehen viele Leute gern schwimmen.

4 **Mein neues Zimmer** Choose the logical prepositions to complete Ben's description of his room.

(1) _____ (An / In / Zwischen) meinem neuen Zimmer gibt es viel Platz. Meine Gitarre stelle ich

gleich (2) _____ (an / auf / über) die Wand. (3) _____ (Vor / Zwischen / In) das Fenster stelle

ich mein neues Fahrrad. (4) _____ (Auf / Unter / Neben) das Fahrrad stelle ich einen Stuhl.

(5) _____ (In / Vor / Auf) dem Stuhl ist schon ein Papierkorb. Meine große Vase steht (6) _____

(zwischen / über / in) Stuhl und Papierkorb. Der Schreibtisch steht auch (7) _____ (am / im / vor)

Zimmer. (8) _____ (Zwischen / Über / Unter) dem Schreibtisch schläft die Katze. (9) _____

(In / Über / Unter) dem Schreibtisch hängt eine blaue Lampe. Ein Foto von meiner Freundin steht immer

(10) _____ (hinter / auf / unter) dem Schreibtisch. Das Bett steht (11) _____ (neben / in / auf)

der Tür. (12) _____ (Zwischen / Auf / Über) dem Bett liegt mein Buch.

5 **Was fehlt?** Provide the definite articles in the accusative or dative.

1. Die Band spielt heute Abend in _____ Konzert.

2. Wir gehen morgen in _____ Konditorei.

3. Sie suchen Herrn Hartmann? Er sitzt dort drüben auf _____ Stuhl zwischen

   _____ Professoren.

4. Alexandra und Greta warten schon lange in _____ Restaurant.

5. Frau Peters fährt das Auto vor _____ Schule. Ihre Kinder warten schon in

   _____ Sporthalle.

6. Die Schüler legen das Geld auf _____ Schreibtisch.

7. Ich habe die Eier neben _____ Kartoffeln gelegt.

8. Er hat das Buch auf _____ Tisch gelegt. Es liegt jetzt auf _____

   Tisch neben _____ Vase.

6 **Wo machen wir was?** Answer with complete sentences.

1. Wohin können wir Pizza essen gehen?

   _____

2. Wo wandern Sie gern?

   _____

3. Wohin gehen die Studenten zum Mittagessen?

   _____

4. Wo kann ich einen heißen Kaffee kaufen?

   _____

5. Wohin sollen die Gäste ihre Autos stellen?

   _____

6. Wo lernen Sie Fremdsprachen?

   _____

Kapitel 2 Lektion 2A

KONTEXT

1 **Möbel oder Zimmer?** Sort the words into categories.

das Arbeitszimmer	der Dachboden	der Keller	das Schlafzimmer
das Badezimmer	der Esstisch	die Kommode	der Schreibtisch
das Bett	das Esszimmer	die Küche	der Sessel
das Bild	der Flur	die Lampe	das Sofa
das Bücherregal	die Garage	der Nachttisch	das Wohnzimmer

Möbel	Zimmer

2 **Was passt?** Match the words in the left column with the description of what happens there.

1. _____ die Küche
2. _____ das Badezimmer
3. _____ das Schlafzimmer
4. _____ die Garage
5. _____ das Wohnzimmer
6. _____ das Esszimmer
7. _____ das Arbeitszimmer

a. Da schlafe ich.
b. Dort macht Opa das Abendessen.
c. Dort parke ich das Auto.
d. Hier arbeite ich am Computer.
e. Hier gehe ich in die Badewanne.
f. Hier ist unser Fernseher.
g. Wir essen hier zusammen.

3 **Was ist das?** Choose the word that best describes the picture.

die Badewanne	das Bücherregal	die Kommode	der Schreibtisch	der Teppich
das Bett	der Esstisch	die Lampe	das Sofa	der Vorhang

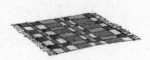

1. _____ 2. _____ 3. _____ 4. _____

5. _____ 6. _____ 7. _____ 8. _____

Kapitel 2 Workbook Activities **17**

Workbook

4   **Das Haus**   Name the objects in the picture below.

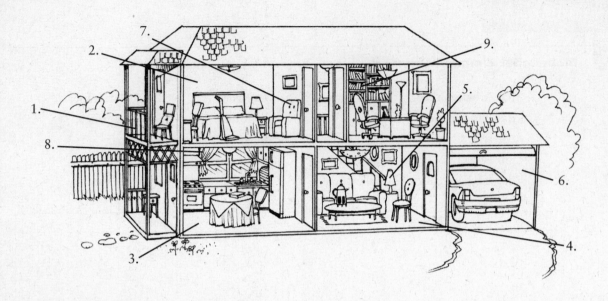

1. _____

2. _____

3. _____

4. _____

5. _____

6. _____

7. _____

8. _____

9. _____

5   **Schreiben**   Name five things you have in your room and five things you don't.

Beispiel

> In meinem Zimmer habe ich ein Bett, einen Tisch, eine Lampe,...
> In meinem Zimmer habe ich keinen Esstisch, keine Badewanne,...

_____

_____

_____

_____

_____

_____

STRUKTUREN

2A.1 The *Präteritum*

1 **Präsens oder Präteritum?** Choose the correct tense.

	Präsens	Präteritum
1. Wir waren zusammen in Berlin.	○	○
2. Tante Maria schenkte mir Blumen zum Geburtstag.	○	○
3. Sie warten auf unseren Professor.	○	○
4. Er geht zum Fußballspiel.	○	○
5. Klara mochte das neue Kleid.	○	○
6. Großvater kochte uns ein leckeres Abendessen.	○	○
7. Ich fahre am Dienstag nach Mainz.	○	○
8. Hattest du am Montag frei?	○	○

2 **Was fehlt?** Fill in the missing verb forms in the **Präteritum**.

	1. lachen	2. kaufen	3. sehen	4. bringen	5. mieten	6. bleiben
ich				brachte		
du		kauftest				
er/sie/es						blieb
wir	lachten					
ihr					mietetet	
Sie/sie			sahen			

3 **Bilden Sie Sätze** Write sentences in the **Präteritum**.

> **Beispiel**
> ich / sein / in der Küche
> Ich war in der Küche.

1. Anna / kennen / meinen Onkel / sehr gut

_____

2. die Vorhänge / kosten / zu viel

_____

3. Jan / sitzen / auf dem Sofa

_____

4. ihr / wollen / nach Hause

_____

5. du / machen / deine Hausaufgaben / zu spät

_____

6. die Familie / reisen / nach Paris

_____

Workbook

4 **Was ist passiert?** Rewrite the sentences using the **Präteritum**.

> **Beispiel**
> Anna geht die Treppe hinauf.
> *Anna ging die Treppe hinauf.*

1. Tim sieht Sara vor dem Haus.
   _____

2. Wir können den großen Schrank nicht ins Zimmer stellen.
   _____

3. Du spielst mit den Katzen von Familie Heuser.
   _____

4. Die neue Wohnung gefällt mir sehr.
   _____

5. Ich studiere Deutsch.
   _____

6. Die Teller fallen auf den Boden.
   _____

5 **Bilder beschreiben** Describe the activities using the **Präteritum**.

> **Beispiel**
> das Kind / fahren / mit dem Fahrrad
> *Das Kind fuhr mit dem Fahrrad.*

1. die Frau / laufen / früh am Morgen

2. Frau Zimmermann / lesen / ein Buch

3. sie / tanzen / zusammen in der Disko

4. die Bäckerin / backen / Pizza

5. Tobias / trinken / Wasser aus der Flasche

1. _____
2. _____
3. _____
4. _____
5. _____

Workbook

2A.2 *Da-, wo-, hin-,* and *her-*compounds

1 **Was passt?** Choose the appropriate compound to complete the sentence.

1. (Woher / Daher) kommst du?

2. Was steht vor dem Fenster? Das Bücherregal steht (davor / wovor).

3. Die Kinder sind sehr ruhig. (Damit / Womit) spielen sie?

4. Der Hund ist im Garten, aber Max lässt ihn (herein / heraus).

5. Opa kommt die Treppe vom ersten Stock ins Erdgeschoss (herauf / herunter).

6. (Wohin / Woher) gehen wir am Wochenende, nach Zürich?

2 **Fragen** Use **wo**-compounds to write questions about the underlined part of each sentence.

> **Beispiel**
>
> Die Vase steht *dort auf dem Tisch.*
> *Wo steht die Vase?*

> ~~wo~~   wofür   wohin   womit   woraus   worüber

1. Tobias geht <u>in den Keller.</u>

   _____

2. Opa Peter spricht mit seiner Enkeltochter <u>über das Wetter.</u>

   _____

3. Mutter hat einen Nachtisch <u>aus Schokolade</u> gemacht.

   _____

4. Greta braucht ein neues Kleid <u>für den Strand.</u>

   _____

5. Am Wochenende muss Lisa <u>mit dem Bus</u> fahren.

   _____

3 **Antworten** Answer each question with a **da**-compound or a prepositional phrase.

> **Beispiel**
>
> Sitzt der Vater auf dem Sofa?
> *Ja, der Vater sitzt darauf.*

1. Schreibt der Junge am Computer?

   _____

2. Sitzt das Mädchen neben ihrem Vater?

   _____

3. Liegen die Fotos unter dem Tisch?

   _____

4. Liegen die Fotos auf dem Tisch?

   _____

5. Spricht der Junge mit seiner Schwester?

   _____

Workbook

4 **Fragen und Antworten** Match the questions on the left with the answers on the right.

1. Worüber spricht die Lehrerin?
2. Woher kommt Emma?
3. Wohin geht ihr jetzt?
4. Kommt David herunter?
5. Wofür dankt die Frau ihrem Mann?

a. _____ Nein, er geht hinauf.
b. _____ Sie spricht über die Schweiz.
c. _____ Sie dankt ihm für die Geburtstagskarte.
d. _____ Wir gehen jetzt in den Park.
e. _____ Sie kommt aus England.

5 **Der Detektiv** Complete this dialogue between a detective and a witness. Not all words will be used.

dafür	damit	davor
dagegen	danach	wohin
dahin	darüber	womit

DETEKTIV Wo waren Sie am Freitagabend, Frau Meyer?

FRAU MEYER Am Freitagnachmittag bin ich ins Konzert gegangen.

DETEKTIV (1) _____ sind Sie vor dem Konzert gegangen?

FRAU MEYER Vor dem Konzert? (2) _____ war ich im Restaurant.

DETEKTIV Und (3) _____? Was haben sie nach dem Konzert gemacht?

FRAU MEYER Ich bin nach Hause gefahren.

DETEKTIV Sind Sie sicher? Sie sind nicht in die Kneipe gegangen?

FRAU MEYER Ganz sicher nicht! Ich gehe nicht (4) _____.

DETEKTIV (5) _____ sind Sie nach Hause gefahren? Mit dem Auto?

FRAU MEYER Nein, (6) _____ bin ich nicht gefahren. Ich bin mit dem Fahrrad gefahren.

DETEKTIV Ihre Antworten haben mir sehr geholfen. Ich danke Ihnen (7) _____.

6 **Ein Interview** Choose a famous person, write five questions to ask that person, and create responses.

Beispiel

Frage: Frau J.K. Rowling, woher kommen Sie?
Antwort: Ich komme aus Gloucestershire in England.

1. Frage: _____
   Antwort: _____

2. Frage: _____
   Antwort: _____

3. Frage: _____
   Antwort: _____

4. Frage: _____
   Antwort: _____

5. Frage: _____
   Antwort: _____

2A.3 Coordinating conjunctions

Workbook

1 **Was passt?** Select the most logical coordinating conjunction.

1. Auf dem Balkon las ich ein Buch, (aber / denn) dort war es schön und warm.

2. Anna ist meine Nachbarin (und / oder) eine gute Freundin.

3. Die Wohnung gefällt uns, (sondern / aber) sie ist sehr klein.

4. Sie können Kaffee (und / oder) Tee zum Frühstück trinken.

5. Ich brachte einen Regenschirm mit, (und / denn) es hat stark geregnet.

6. Am Sonntag sind wir nicht spazieren gegangen, (sondern / aber) ans Meer gefahren.

7. Sie wollte das Stück Kuchen nicht nehmen, (sondern / denn) sie ist auf Diät.

2 **Was fehlt?** Choose the appropriate coordinating conjunction from the list.

aber   denn   oder   sondern   und

1. Sie kaufte keinen Sessel, _____ einen Tisch für ihr Wohnzimmer.

2. Wir wollen heute Abend auf die Party gehen, _____ morgen müssen wir früh aufstehen.

3. Am Tag studiert er an der Universität _____ am Abend arbeitet er im Lebensmittelgeschäft.

4. Er ist müde und geht früh ins Bett, _____ er hat seit dem frühen Morgen gearbeitet.

5. Wir können die Kommode in dein Zimmer _____ in mein Zimmer stellen.

3 **Ergänzen Sie** Complete each sentence with a logical conjunction and a statement from the list.

Die Großeltern kommen zu Besuch.   Es will mit den anderen Kindern im Garten spielen.
Er will meinen Geburtstag feiern.   ~~Übermorgen ist Wochenende.~~
Es ist schon dunkel.   Wir können Tennis spielen.

Beispiel
Heute ist Donnerstag und übermorgen ist Wochenende.

1. Es ist erst 18 Uhr, _____.

2. Nächste Woche ist Weihnachten, _____.

3. Das Kind will nicht hineinkommen, _____.

4. Max kommt mit mir ins Restaurant, _____.

5. Wir können einkaufen gehen, _____.

Kapitel 2 Workbook Activities   **23**

4   **Im Wohnzimmer** Use the image to complete the sentences with logical coordinating conjunctions: aber, denn, oder, sondern, und.

Martin — Sophia — Johanna — Manfred
Bello — Tobias

1. Martin sitzt auf dem Sofa neben Sophia _____ spielt mit dem Hund Bello.

2. Tobias kann das Buch in seiner Hand _____ das Buch auf dem Boden lesen.

3. Opa Manfred braucht eine Brille, _____ seine Augen sind müde.

4. Sophia spricht mit Johanna, _____ Martin hört nicht zu.

5. Tobias sitzt nicht auf dem Sofa, _____ auf dem Boden.

5   **So wohne ich** Describe your home using a coordinating conjunction in each sentence.

> *Beispiel*
>
> Wir wohnen nicht in einem Haus, sondern in einer Wohnung. Ich habe eine große Lampe im Wohnzimmer und eine kleine Lampe im Schlafzimmer.

_____

_____

_____

_____

_____

6   **Sätze schreiben** Use the vocabulary from the chapter to write sentences about your life at home. Use a coordinating conjunction in each sentence.

> *Beispiel*
>
> Ich koche gern in der Küche, aber mein Mann kocht auch.
> Abends lese ich ein Buch auf dem Sofa, denn im Bett werde ich müde.

1. _____

2. _____

3. _____

4. _____

5. _____

Workbook

Kapitel 2

Lektion 2B

KONTEXT

1 **Hausarbeiten** Indicate whether each sentence is **logisch** or **unlogisch**.

		logisch	unlogisch
1.	Julia fegt mit einem Besen.	○	○
2.	Sebastian putzte das Geschirr.	○	○
3.	Sie trockneten die Bettdecken im Herd.	○	○
4.	Er deckt den Tisch zum Mittagessen.	○	○
5.	Sie wischt die Fenster mit dem Staubsauger ab.	○	○
6.	Wir waschen die Wäsche in der Waschmaschine.	○	○

2 **Oma kommt zu Besuch** Choose the appliance that fits the task.

1. _____ Erst backen wir einen Kuchen für Oma.   a. die Spülmaschine

2. _____ Dann kochen wir den Kaffee.   b. der Kühlschrank

3. _____ Wir decken den Tisch damit.   c. der Ofen

4. _____ Das Geschirr ist jetzt schmutzig.   d. die Kaffeemaschine

5. _____ Wir stellen die Milch dorthin.   e. das Geschirr

3 **Was passt zusammen?** Match each word with its description, and then write a sentence with that word.

> **Beispiel**
>
> _a_ Was müssen wir tun? Hier ist ein Saustall!
> Wir müssen aufräumen.

_____ 1. Ich mache den Boden mit einem Besen sauber.   a. aufräumen

_____ 2. Lena hat das Bügeleisen.   b. bügeln

_____ 3. Ben braucht saubere Wäsche.   c. fegen

_____ 4. Nils will den Teppich saubermachen.   d. staubsaugen

_____ 5. Greta stellt die sauberen Teller in den Schrank.   e. wegräumen

        f. waschen

1. _____

2. _____

3. _____

4. _____

5. _____

Workbook

4 **Was fehlt?** Complete the dialogue in which Frau Müller interviews a cleaning service. Not all words will be used.

entfernen	schmutzig	waschen
fegen	spülen	Waschmaschine
Kühlschrank	Spülmaschine	wischen
sauber	Staubsauger	

FRAU MÜLLER Guten Tag! Ich möchte Ihnen ein paar Fragen stellen. Haben Sie schon mal eine (1) _____ für das Geschirr benutzt?

REINIGUNGSKRAFT Oh ja! Aber ich (2) _____ das Porzellan immer in der Spüle.

FRAU MÜLLER Benutzen Sie einen (3) _____ oder einen Besen für den Boden?

REINIGUNGSKRAFT Wenn er nicht sehr (4) _____ ist, benutze ich einen Besen.

FRAU MÜLLER Wie (5) _____ Sie Staub?

REINIGUNGSKRAFT Ich (6) _____ Staub mit einem Staubtuch (*cloth*).

5 **Was machen sie?** Write a sentence describing each of these household chores.

Beispiel

Er fegt den Boden.

1.   2.   3.

1. _____

2. _____

3. _____

6 **Dialog** Write a short dialogue in which you and your roommate discuss how to divide up the housework.

_____

_____

_____

_____

_____

_____

STRUKTUREN

2B.1 *Perfekt* versus *Präteritum*

1   **Perfekt oder Präteritum?** Indicate if the verb in each sentence is in **Perfekt** or **Präteritum**.

	Perfekt	Präteritum
1. Ich musste den Müll rausbringen.	○	○
2. Habt ihr Fußball gespielt?	○	○
3. Daniel hat mir alles aufgeschrieben.	○	○
4. Er arbeitete am Nachmittag in der Garage.	○	○
5. Der Hund rannte im Park herum.	○	○
6. Sie waren am Wochenende in Luzern.	○	○
7. Erik putzte die Wohnung.	○	○
8. Anna hat den Staubsauger in den Keller getragen.	○	○

2   **Was fehlt?** Complete the table with the missing information.

	Infinitiv	Präteritum	Partizip
1.		fuhr	
2.			gedacht
3.	waschen		
4.			getroffen
5.		trank	
6.	erklären		

3   **Anders gesagt** Rewrite the following sentences in the **Präteritum**.

> **Beispiel**
> Du hast den Boden gefegt.
> *Du fegtest den Boden.*

1. Mutter hat uns einen leckeren Kuchen gebacken.

   _____

2. Julius hat in der Küche das Geschirr gespült.

   _____

3. Ich habe die Wäsche aus dem Trockner genommen.

   _____

4. Paula hat die Betten für uns gemacht.

   _____

    Kapitel 2 Workbook Activities   **27**

4 **Was habt ihr gemacht?** Write sentences in the **Perfekt** using the cues.

> **Beispiel**
> Lukas / Boden / wischen
> Lukas hat den Boden gewischt.

1. Vater / Tisch / decken

   _____

2. Fabian / Wäsche / bügeln

   _____

3. er / Toilette / putzen

   _____

4. wir / Geschirr / spülen

   _____

5. Nina / Boden / fegen

   _____

5 **Dialog** Write a short dialogue in which George and Sabite talk about all the chores they did this week. Use the **Perfekt** and the **Präteritum** appropriately. Choose from the verbs below.

bügeln	putzen	wischen
fegen	waschen	

GEORGE <u>Wir waren diese Woche sehr fleißig</u>!

SABITE _____

GEORGE _____

SABITE _____

GEORGE _____

SABITE _____

GEORGE _____

SABITE _____

GEORGE _____

SABITE _____

6 **Erzählen Sie** Write an e-mail to a friend about your weekend, using the **Perfekt** and the **Präteritum**.

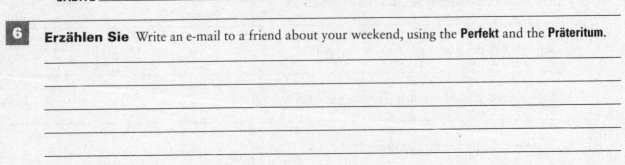

_____

_____

_____

_____

_____

2B.2 Separable and inseparable prefix verbs (*Perfekt*)

1 **Ein Rätsel** Write the past participle of each verb, and then find it in the puzzle.

1. abstauben _____

2. einkaufen _____

3. einschlafen _____

4. empfehlen _____

5. entschließen _____

6. gewinnen _____

7. mitbringen _____

8. mitkommen _____

9. verkaufen _____

10. verschmutzen _____

```
W  X  H  W  A  G  O  X  S  A  G  O  R  M  A
M  S  V  Y  E  J  E  M  A  H  V  N  S  I  B
I  E  U  E  F  Q  K  W  I  S  R  E  P  M  G
T  I  E  X  R  C  O  T  O  X  E  I  H  I  E
G  N  N  G  W  K  F  W  V  N  S  N  N  T  S
E  G  H  E  T  S  A  E  E  T  N  G  C  G  T
K  E  D  G  M  I  O  U  P  E  I  E  H  E  A
O  S  K  L  I  P  B  X  F  Q  V  K  N  B  U
M  C  T  I  M  P  F  E  Y  T  E  A  N  R  B
M  H  A  E  X  N  M  O  G  Z  R  U  D  A  T
E  L  F  G  E  V  E  R  H  E  M  F  T  C  A
N  A  T  E  M  L  G  R  O  L  N  T  D  H  F
T  F  F  U  J  L  T  H  U  M  E  K  Q  T  H
V  E  R  S  C  H  M  U  T  Z  T  N  C  M  I
E  N  T  S  C  H  L  O  S  S  E  N  S  B  X
```

2 **Aufräumen** Complete the sentences with the **Perfekt** of the verbs in parentheses.

Simon und Max haben gestern das Haus (1) _____ (aufräumen). Simon hat mit dem

Wohnzimmer (2) _____ (anfangen). Max hat in der Küche das Geschirr aus der Spülmaschine

(3) _____ (wegräumen). Im Flur hat Simon (4) _____ (staubsaugen). Nach dem

Aufräumen haben beide den Müll (5) _____ (rausbringen). Danach hat Simon die trockene

Wäsche (6) _____ (bügeln). Die Eltern sind dann zu Hause (7) _____ (ankommen),

und die Familie ist zum Abendessen (8) _____ (ausgehen). Die Jungen haben ein gutes Essen

(9) _____ (bestellen).

3 **Was fehlt?** Complete the sentences using the **Perfekt** of the given verbs.

1. Nach dem Essen _____ die Kinder _____. (ausgehen)

2. Marie _____ den Verkäufer _____. (verstehen)

3. Ich _____ in die neue Wohnung _____. (umziehen)

4. Gestern _____ ihr früh _____. (aufstehen)

5. Felix _____ noch nicht seine Hausaufgaben _____. (anfangen)

Workbook

Workbook

4 **Was passiert hier?** Describe what has happened using the **Perfekt** and the words provided.

(Jasmin / einen Kaffee / bestellen)
Jasmin hat einen Kaffee bestellt.

1. (Jana / ihren Freund / anrufen) _____ _____

2. (Lisa / im Supermarkt / einkaufen) _____

3. (Mia / auf dem Sofa / einschlafen) _____

4. (wir / ein leckeres Essen / vorbereiten) _____

5. (Freunde / uns zum Picknick / einladen) _____

5 **Einkaufsbummel** Write an e-mail to a friend about a recent shopping trip. Use the **Perfekt** of six of the verbs provided.

ausgehen	einkaufen	umtauschen
bestellen	entdecken	vergessen
bezahlen	erklären	verkaufen

Lieber Martin / Liebe Anna, am Montag habe ich in Düsseldorf eingekauft. Ich...

_____

_____

_____

_____

6 **Mein tolles Wochenende** Tell a family member all that you did last weekend. Provide as much detail as possible. Use verbs with prefixes.

1. Am Freitagabend: _____

2. Samstagmorgen: _____

3. Am Abend: _____

4. Sonntag früh: _____

5. Sonntagabend: _____

Kapitel 3

KONTEXT

1 **Die Monate** Complete the listing of the seasons with the names of the missing months.

1. Sommer: Juni, _____ , August

2. Herbst: September, _____ , November

3. Winter: _____ , Januar, _____

4. Frühling: _____ , April, _____

2 **Wie ist das Wetter?** Match the weather description to the picture it describes.

a. 8° C

b. 25° C

c. 31° C

d. –2° C

e. 2° C

f. 33° C

1. _____ Die Sonne scheint und es ist sehr warm.

2. _____ Es ist kühl und wolkig.

3. _____ Es ist kalt und windig.

4. _____ Es ist ziemlich warm und es regnet.

5. _____ Es schneit.

6. _____ Es ist sehr heiß und es kommt ein starker Sturm.

3 **Die Jahreszeiten** Name the season or seasons in which you are most likely to find these weather conditions or do these activities.

1. Es ist furchtbar heiß. _____

2. Es ist kalt und schneit. _____

3. Man braucht oft einen Regenmantel. _____

4. Es ist sonnig und wir gehen oft schwimmen. _____

5. Wir gehen Skifahren. _____

6. Wir feiern Halloween. _____

4 **Logisch oder unlogisch?** For each pair of statements, decide whether the second statement follows logically from the first.

	logisch	unlogisch
1. Heute gibt es überall Nebel. Man kann sehr weit sehen.	○	○
2. Der Sturm bringt Hagel und Blitz. Das ist kein Wetter für einen Spaziergang!	○	○
3. Es wird kühl. Ich glaube, ich ziehe eine Jacke an.	○	○
4. Es ist Mitte März. Der Herbst beginnt.	○	○
5. Heute schneit es. Ich ziehe eine kurze Hose an.	○	○
6. Ich habe im April Geburtstag. Ich bin ein Frühlingskind.	○	○

5 **Was fehlt?** Complete each statement with the appropriate noun.

> **Beispiel**
> Es war sonnig, aber jetzt ist die Sonne hinter einer Wolke.

1. Eine _____ hat sieben Tage.

2. Ein _____ hat zwischen 28 und 31 Tagen.

3. Ein _____ hat 365 Tage.

4. Wenn es schneit, liegt _____ auf dem Boden.

5. Ich sehe zuerst den Blitz und dann höre ich den _____ .

6 **Jahreszeiten** Write an email to a German friend in which you explain what your favorite season is and why. Describe what the weather is like in that season where you live.

> **Beispiel**
> Liebe Hanna / Lieber Jonas,
> meine Lieblingsjahreszeit ist ...

_____

_____

_____

_____

_____

_____

_____

_____

_____

_____

Workbook

STRUKTUREN

3A.1 Separable and inseparable prefix verbs (*Präteritum*)

1 Marias Tag Complete the summary of Maria's day with the appropriate separable prefixes.

an	auf	aus	ein	mit	zurück

1. Maria stand um acht Uhr _____.

2. Sie zog Jeans und einen Pulli _____.

3. Sie nahm einen Regenschirm _____.

4. Sie kam abends um neun _____.

5. Sie zog sich _____.

6. Um zehn schlief sie _____.

2 Was fehlt? Complete the narrative about Niklas using verbs from the list in the **Präteritum**.

anfangen	erklären	verbringen
anrufen	mitbringen	verstehen

1. Das Herbstsemester _____ letzte Woche _____.

2. Niklas _____ gestern den ganzen Tag in der Bibliothek.

3. Er _____ die Physikhausaufgaben nicht.

4. Am Abend _____ er seine Freundin Alexandra _____.

5. Alexandra kam zur Bibliothek und _____ das Physikbuch _____.

6. Sie _____ Niklas die Hausaufgaben.

3 Letzten Sommer Write complete sentences in the **Präteritum** using the cues.

> **Beispiel**
>
> letzten Sommer / besuchen / wir / meine Verwandten in Deutschland
> *Letzten Sommer besuchten wir meine Verwandten in Deutschland.*

1. meine Eltern / mitbringen / viele Geschenke

_____

2. wir / ankommen / morgens um elf

_____

3. meine Tante / einladen / uns / zum Abendessen

_____

4. wir / fernsehen / danach

_____

5. ich / verstehen / ziemlich viel

_____

Workbook

4 **Was machten sie gestern?** Write a sentence in the **Präteritum** about each picture using expressions from the list.

 Peter

Beispiel

Peter sah den ganzen Abend fern.

ihre Freundin anrufen	einen Film anschauen	ihren Opa besuchen
das Essen vorbereiten	elegante Kleider anziehen	einen Kaffee bestellen

1. David

2. Florian

3. Anna

4. Nils und Lisa

5. Emma

6. Herr und Frau Bauer

1. _____

2. _____

3. _____

4. _____

5. _____

6. _____

5 **Wie war's damals?** Write about something you had to do, did or did not want to do, or were allowed or not allowed to do. Use the **Präteritum** of **dürfen**, **müssen**, or **wollen** with verbs from the list.

Beispiel

Gestern musste ich für die Matheprüfung lernen.

anziehen	ausgehen	mitbringen
aufräumen	besuchen	übernachten
aufstehen	fernsehen	verbringen

1. Gestern _____.

2. Vorgestern _____.

3. Letztes Wochenende _____.

4. Letztes Semester _____.

3A.2 Prepositions of location; Prepositions in set phrases

1 **Was passt?** Choose the correct preposition.

1. Hast du Angst (von / vor / mit) Blitz und Donner?

2. Ich denke oft (an / auf / vor) meine Zeit in Deutschland.

3. Warum hast du nicht (bei / auf / nach) meine Frage geantwortet?

4. Lisa arbeitet (auf / bei / an) ihrem Referat.

5. Das Buch handelt (von / in / mit) ihrer Kindheit in Afrika.

6. Hast du lange (nach / mit / auf) den Bus gewartet?

7. Wohnst du noch (an / in / auf) der Goethestraße?

8. Schreibst du oft E-Mails (in / an / nach) deine Freunde?

9. Mein Onkel wohnt (auf / an / in) der Schweiz.

2 **Was ist richtig?** Complete the narrative by choosing an appropriate ending for each sentence.

1. Ich denke oft _____

2. Meine Oma hat als Kind _____

3. Sie erzählt gern _____

4. Ihr Haus lag direkt _____

5. Jedes Wochenende kaufte ihre Mutter _____

6. Ich will jetzt einen Brief _____

a. an einem kleinen See.

b. an meine Oma.

c. in der Schweiz gewohnt.

d. an meine Oma schreiben.

e. auf dem Markt ein.

f. von ihrer Kindheit in der Schweiz.

3 **Präpositionen** Complete each sentence with a preposition of location.

1. Die Uhr hängt _____ der Wand.

2. _____ dem Markt kaufen wir frisches Gemüse.

3. In den Sommerferien wohnt Alex _____ seinen Eltern.

4. Wir wohnen _____ der Ringstraße.

5. Neustadt liegt _____ der Ostsee.

6. Hast du Hunger? Das Essen steht schon _____ dem Tisch.

7. _____ der Wand hängt ein tolles Poster von Berlin.

8. Meine Katze schläft gern _____ dem Balkon in der Sonne.

9. Kaufst du gern _____ Aldi ein?

Kapitel 3 Workbook Activities

4 **Beschreiben Sie das Bild** Write a description of what is happening in the classroom using phrases from the list.

> **Beispiel**
> Die Schüler warten auf ihren Lehrer.

antworten auf	reden über
erzählen von	schreiben an
fragen nach	sitzen auf
helfen bei	stehen in
lachen über	~~warten auf~~

1. _____

2. _____

3. _____

4. _____

5. _____

6. _____

5 **Persönliche Fragen** Answer the questions in complete sentences.

1. Wovor haben Sie Angst?

_____

2. Worüber reden Sie gern?

_____

3. Worüber reden Sie nicht gern?

_____

4. Woran arbeiten Sie im Moment?

_____

5. An wen denken Sie oft?

_____

6. Wie oft helfen Sie bei der Hausarbeit?

_____

7. Wovon handelt Ihr Lieblingsbuch?

_____

Workbook

Kapitel 3

Lektion 3B

KONTEXT

1 **Was passt?** Match each word with its definition.

_____ 1. das Gepäck   a. eine Schiffsreise auf dem Meer

_____ 2. der Personalausweis b. was man auf eine Reise mitbringt

_____ 3. der Schlüssel   c. hier kann man einen Flug buchen

_____ 4. das Reisebüro   d. eine Identitätskarte

_____ 5. die Kreuzfahrt   e. damit kommt man in die höheren Stockwerke

_____ 6. der Fahrstuhl   f. damit öffnet man eine Tür

2 **Am Flughafen** Indicate whether each noun is something you could find in an airport or not.

	am Flughafen	nicht am Flughafen
1. das Meer	○	○
2. der Koffer	○	○
3. die Bordkarte	○	○
4. die Kreuzfahrt	○	○
5. der Passagier	○	○
6. der Strand	○	○
7. der Zimmerservice	○	○
8. der Zoll	○	○

3 **Wo hört man das?** Read the following statements and choose the most logical place you might hear them.

_____ 1. Wir haben ein ausgezeichnetes Restaurant hier im Haus, aber vielleicht möchten Sie lieber Zimmerservice.

a. am Zoll

b. im Fünf-Sterne-Hotel

_____ 2. Könnten Sie bitte auf die 3 drücken? Ich möchte in den 3. Stock.

c. am Flughafen

_____ 3. Ja, hier können wir sehr billig übernachten, aber wir müssen ein Zimmer mit anderen teilen.

d. in der Jugendherberge

e. im Reisebüro

_____ 4. Den Koffer dürfen Sie leider nicht als Handgepäck mit an Bord nehmen. Er ist viel zu groß.

f. im Fahrstuhl

_____ 5. Wir möchten einen Urlaub in Italien buchen.

_____ 6. Das frische Obst dürfen Sie leider nicht mitnehmen.

4 **Urlaubspläne** Complete the dialogue using words from the list. Not all words will be used.

buchen	Jugendherberge	Meer	übernachten
Gepäck	Kreuzfahrt	Skiurlaub	voll besetzt
Hotel	landen	Strand	Zimmerservice

JULIAN Vielleicht können wir in den Ferien einen (1) _____ in den Alpen machen.

ANNIKA Fahren wir doch ans (2) _____, denn ich schwimme so gern und liege sehr gern den ganzen Tag am (3) _____! Wir brauchen auch weniger Kleider und müssen nicht so viel (4) _____ mitnehmen.

JULIAN Na gut, dann (5) _____ wir einen Flug nach Mallorca. Ich kenne ein tolles (6) Fünf-Sterne-_____ dort. Hoffentlich ist es noch nicht (7) _____.

ANNIKA Ach, ich möchte den Urlaub lieber in einer (8) _____ verbringen. Da kann man billiger (9) _____ und es macht mehr Spaß.

JULIAN Aber dort gibt es keinen (10) _____!

ANNIKA So was ist nicht so wichtig! Ich esse sowieso viel lieber im Restaurant.

5 **Gespräch am Flughafen** Choose two people from the picture and imagine they strike up a conversation as they are waiting for their flights. Write the dialogue between them.

_____

_____

_____

_____

_____

_____

6 **Eine Postkarte aus dem Urlaub** You are taking your dream vacation. Write a postcard describing your trip: how you got there, where you are staying, and what you are doing.

_____

_____

_____

_____

_____

_____

STRUKTUREN

3B.1 Infinitive expressions and clauses

1   **Was passt?** Choose the word that best fits the context.

1. (Anstatt / Ohne / Um) mit dem Zug zu fahren, fliegen wir nach Paris.
2. Klara geht zum Reisebüro, (anstatt / ohne / um) eine Kreuzfahrt zu buchen.
3. Du kannst nicht ins Ausland fahren, (anstatt / ohne / um) durch die Passkontrolle zu gehen.
4. (Anstatt / Ohne / Um) pünktlich anzukommen, müssen wir jetzt abfahren.
5. Fahr nicht zum Strand, (anstatt / ohne / um) eine Sonnenbrille einzupacken.
6. Wir mussten lange Schlange stehen, (anstatt / ohne / um) die Tickets zu bekommen.
7. Gehen Sie nicht aus dem Haus, (anstatt / ohne / um) den Schlüssel mitzunehmen.
8. (Anstatt / Ohne / Um) Zimmerservice zu bestellen, geht Florian ins Restaurant.

2   **Skiurlaub** Choose the appropriate infinitive clause to complete each sentence in the narrative.

1. Ich fliege heute nach Österreich, _____   a. an Bord zu gehen.
2. Ich habe aber leider vergessen, _____   b. um Ski zu fahren.
3. Ich habe jetzt keine Zeit, _____   c. anstatt jetzt nach Hause zu fahren.
4. Die Passagiere beginnen, _____   d. wieder nach Hause zu fahren.
5. Ich werde eine neue Jacke in Österreich kaufen, _____   e. meine Skijacke mitzubringen.
6. Ich werde nie wieder in Urlaub gehen, _____   f. ohne meine Jacke einzupacken.

3   **Bilden Sie Sätze** Complete each sentence using the **zu** expression in parentheses with the most logical phrase from the word bank.

Beispiel

Man braucht viel Geld, <u>um einen Mercedes zu kaufen</u>. (um... zu).

ins Restaurant gehen	ein Zimmer in diesem Hotel bekommen
mit Kreditkarte bezahlen	~~einen Mercedes kaufen~~
die Bordkarte zeigen	ins Ausland fahren
die Sprache verstehen	

1. Man darf nicht ins Flugzeug, _____. (ohne...zu)
2. Man braucht einen Pass, _____. (um...zu)
3. Man muss einen Scheck schreiben, _____. (anstatt...zu)
4. Man muss ziemlich früh buchen, _____. (um...zu)
5. Man kann Zimmerservice bestellen, _____. (anstatt...zu)
6. Man kann keine deutsche Zeitung lesen, _____. (ohne...zu)

Kapitel 3 Workbook Activities   **39**

4   **Anstatt** For each pair of pictures, write a sentence describing what these people did instead of what they were supposed to do.

Erik

> **Beispiel**
>
> Anstatt das *Geschirr* zu spülen, hat Erik Fußball *gespielt*.

1. Max

2. Julia

3. Moritz

4. Sophia

1. _____

2. _____

3. _____

4. _____

5   **Was meinen Sie?** Complete the sentences with your own ideas using infinitive clauses with **zu**.

> **Beispiel**
>
> Es macht mir keinen Spaß, *mein Zimmer aufzuräumen*.

1. Es macht mir großen Spaß, _____

2. Ich habe nie Zeit, _____

3. Ich habe jetzt Lust, _____

4. Ich finde es einfach, _____

5. Ich finde es langweilig, _____

3B.2 Time expressions

1 **Was ist richtig?** Choose the best response to each question.

1. Wie lange wohnst du schon in Berlin, Nina?
   a. Dieses Jahr.   b. Vor drei Jahren.   c. Seit zwei Jahren.

2. Wie lange dauert der Flug nach Australien?
   a. Einen Tag.   b. Seit einem Tag.   c. Vor einem Tag.

3. Wie oft fährt der Bus von hier nach Lauterbach?
   a. Am Freitag.   b. Seit einer Woche.   c. Zweimal am Tag.

4. Wann fahren Sie nach Rom?
   a. Schon zwei Wochen.   b. Nächsten Sommer.   c. Zum ersten Mal.

5. Wie oft warst du in der Schweiz?
   a. Nur einmal.   b. Seit einem Jahr.   c. Zuerst.

6. Wie viel Zeit hast du noch?
   a. In einer Stunde.   b. Eine Stunde.   c. Seit einer Stunde.

7. Wann landet das Flugzeug?
   a. In einer Stunde.   b. Noch eine Stunde.   c. Seit einer Stunde.

8. Wann besuchst du deine Oma?
   a. Seit einer Woche.   b. Am Wochenende.   c. Einmal.

2 **Was passt?** Indicate the correct word in each time expression.

1. Ich war vor (einen / einem) Monat in Hamburg.

2. Tim steht schon (eine / einer) Stunde Schlange.

3. Annika hat (der ganze / den ganzen) Tag in der Bibliothek verbracht.

4. Simon geht gern (am / an den) Morgen spazieren.

5. Lara ist seit (eine / einer) Woche krank.

6. (In den / Im) Winter fahre ich oft Ski.

3 **Zeitausdrücke** Complete the sentences with the appropriate time expressions.

einmal	einen Monat	ganze Nacht
letzten Sommer	einer Woche	nächste Woche

1. Wir fliegen _____ im Jahr nach Europa.

2. Jonas wohnt seit _____ in Freiburg.

3. Meine Großeltern fahren _____ in Urlaub.

4. Seine Reise durch Afrika dauerte _____.

5. Ich habe die _____ für meine Chemie-Prüfung gelernt.

6. Michaela war _____ in der Türkei.

Workbook

4 **Persönliche Fragen** Answer in complete sentences.

1. Seit wann kennen Sie Ihre beste Freundin / Ihren besten Freund?

_____

2. Seit wann lernen Sie Deutsch?

_____

3. Seit wann wohnen Sie in dieser Stadt?

_____

4. Wie oft fliegen Sie?

_____

5. Wie oft texten Sie am Tag?

_____

6. Wie oft essen Sie im Restaurant?

_____

7. Wann waren Sie das letzte Mal im Kino?

_____

8. Wann sind Sie zum ersten Mal geflogen?

_____

9. Wie lange haben Sie für Ihre letzte Prüfung gelernt?

_____

5 **Schreiben** Write five sentences about things you have done or plan to do, combining elements from each column.

Beispiel

Vor zwei Tagen bin ich ins Konzert gegangen.
Nächsten Sommer möchte ich einen Job.

A	B
vor	Woche
am	Jahr
im	Tag
in	Wochenende
letzt-	Ferien
nächst-	Sommer
	Freitag

1. _____

2. _____

3. _____

4. _____

5. _____

3B.3 Indefinite pronouns

1 **Was passt?** Choose the appropriate word.

1. (Man / Etwas) braucht einen Pass, um ins Ausland zu fahren.
2. Ich machte die Tür auf, aber (alles / niemand) war da.
3. Das arme Kind hat (man / nichts) gegessen.
4. Hast du (etwas / jemand) von deinen Eltern gehört?
5. Im Deutschkurs muss (man / niemand) natürlich Deutsch sprechen.
6. Ich hoffe, dass (alles / niemand) in meinen Koffer passt.
7. (Etwas / Jemand) hat sein Handgepäck im Flugzeug vergessen.
8. Ich habe mit (niemandem / nichts) darüber gesprochen.

2 **Nils hat Hunger** Complete the paragraph with time expressions from the list.

alles	jemanden	niemand
etwas	man	nichts

Nach seiner Ankunft in Frankfurt hatte Nils großen Hunger und wollte sofort (1) _____ essen. Er hatte aber leider (2) _____ zu essen mitgebracht. Er wollte (3) _____ fragen, wo (4) _____ in der Nähe ein billiges Restaurant finden kann. Er ging zur Information, aber (5) _____ war da. Da sah er vor dem Bahnhof einen kleinen Imbiss und bestellte dort ein Käsebrot und ein Würstchen. Weil er so großen Hunger hatte, aß er (6) _____ sehr schnell auf.

3 **Was kann man hier machen?** Complete the sentences by describing something you can do in each place. Use the indefinite pronoun **man** and the most logical phrase from the word bank.

Beispiel

In der Bibliothek *kann man Bücher lesen*.

andere Touristen kennen lernen	im Sand spielen
~~Bücher lesen~~	Ski fahren
Deutsch lernen	Zimmerservice bestellen
eine Kreuzfahrt buchen	

1. Im Reisebüro _____.
2. In einer Jugendherberge _____.
3. Im Fünf-Sterne-Hotel _____.
4. Im Skiurlaub _____.
5. Am Strand _____.
6. Im Deutschkurs _____.

4 **Bilder beschreiben** Write a sentence about each picture using an impersonal expression from the list. Use your imagination.

> **Beispiel**
>
> Maria will ihrem Freund etwas schreiben.

alles	etwas	jemand
man	nichts	niemand

1.

2.

3.

4.

5.

6.

1. _____

2. _____

3. _____

4. _____

5. _____

6. _____

5 **Reisevorbereitungen** Describe five steps people take when going on a trip. Use the indefinite pronoun **man**.

> **Beispiel**
>
> Zuerst plant man die Reise.
> Dann …

1. Zuerst _____.

2. Dann _____.

3. Danach _____.

4. Zuletzt _____.

Kapitel 4

KONTEXT

Lektion 4A

1 **Was passt nicht?** Choose the word that doesn't belong.

1. die Windschutzscheibe, die Scheinwerfer, der Kofferraum, der Verkehr

2. der Polizist, der Unfall, der Schaffner, der Mechaniker

3. die Tankstelle, das Boot, der LKW, das Taxi

4. der Fahrplan, die Fahrkarte, das Benzin, der Fahrkartenschalter

5. tanken, laufen, parken, reparieren

2 **Was fehlt?** Complete each sentence with the missing word.

1. Der _____ in Berlin ist oft chaotisch.

2. Im Zug kontrolliert der _____ die Fahrkarte.

3. Wenn man nachts fährt, muss man die _____ anmachen.

4. Der Mechaniker _____ das Auto.

5. Bevor man in den Bus darf, muss man die Fahrkarte _____.

6. In Deutschland darf man auf der _____ manchmal schnell fahren.

3 **Was ist das?** Label each of the means of transportation depicted.

1. _____

2. _____

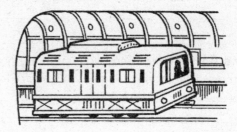

3. _____

4. _____

Workbook

4 **Eine schreckliche Autofahrt** Complete the story with words from the list. Not all the words will be used.

abbiegen	links	Reifen	tanken
Benzin	Mechaniker	reparieren	Tankstelle
bezahlen	Motor	Scheinwerfer	warten
langsam	parken	Sicherheitsgurt	zusammenstoßen

Das Ehepaar Krüger fährt (1) _____ durch die Stadt. Sie haben fast kein

(2) _____ mehr und Herr Krüger sucht eine (3) _____, denn er muss

(4) _____. Plötzlich hört man ein lautes „Pfff" und die Krügers haben einen platten

(5) _____. Herr Krüger muss rechts (6) _____ und das Auto

(7) _____. Ein Polizist steht an der Straße und sagt: „Verkehrskontrolle!" Frau Krüger

hat ihren (8) _____ nicht angelegt und vorne am Auto ist ein (9) _____

kaputt. Die Krügers müssen eine hohe Geldstrafe (10) _____. Der Polizist ist nett

und er ruft einen (11) _____ an. Der kommt sofort und kann das Auto schnell

(12) _____.

5 **Fragen** Answer the questions in complete sentences.

1. Welche Verkehrsmittel benutzen Sie in der Stadt?

   _____

2. Wo müssen Sie oft Schlange stehen?

   _____

3. Hatten Sie schon einmal einen Autounfall?

   _____

4. Entwerten Sie immer Ihre Fahrkarte?

   _____

5. Muss man in Ihrem Land den Sicherheitsgurt anlegen?

   _____

6. Haben Sie letztes Jahr eine lange Zugfahrt gemacht?

   _____

6 **Eine Reise** Write a short account of a trip you took, using the **Perfekt**. Mention at least three modes of transportation and use other vocabulary from this chapter.

_____

_____

_____

_____

_____

_____

STRUKTUREN

4A.1 *Das Plusquamperfekt*

1 **Vor dem Urlaub** The Lange family has gotten ready for vacation. Write complete sentences with the cues provided using the **Plusquamperfekt**.

> **Beispiel**
>
> Familie Lange / zusammen planen / eine Reise
> Familie Lange hatte zusammen eine Reise geplant.

1. Herr Lange / mit dem Auto / zum Mechaniker / gefahren

   _____

2. Frau Lange / das Haus / putzen

   _____

3. die Tochter Julia / auf den Dachboden / klettern

   _____

4. sie / die Koffer / runterbringen

   _____

5. der Sohn Paul / seinen Hamster / zu Freunden / bringen

   _____

6. Frau Lange / die Schlüssel / den Nachbarn / geben

   _____

7. Julia und ihre Mutter / leckere Käsebrote für die Reise / vorbereiten

   _____

8. alle / früh aufstehen

   _____

2 **Der Tag einer Studentin** Complete the sentences using either **nachdem** or **bevor**.

1. _____ ich gefrühstückt hatte, putzte ich mir die Zähne.

2. Ich hatte meine Hausaufgaben eingepackt, _____ ich das Zimmer verließ.

3. Der Lehrer hatte die Tür schon zugemacht, _____ ich ins Klassenzimmer kam.

4. _____ ich die Prüfung geschrieben hatte, traf ich mich mit meinen Freunden.

5. _____ wir am Abend ins Kino gingen, hatten wir mit dem Baseballteam trainiert.

6. _____ der Film anfing, hatten wir uns Popcorn gekauft.

7. Wir kauften uns noch ein leckeres Eis, _____ wir den Film gesehen hatten.

8. Ich ging ins Bett, _____ ich mich von meinen Freunden verabschiedet hatte.

3 **Was fehlt?** Complete the sentences with the cues provided using **nachdem** and the **Plusquamperfekt**.

Beispiel

die Gäste / 100 Hamburger / essen
Nachdem die Gäste 100 Hamburger gegessen hatten, hatten sie endlich keinen Hunger mehr.

1. sie (*pl.*) / viel Wasser und Saft / trinken
_____, waren sie endlich nicht mehr durstig.

2. die Polizei / kommen
_____, machten die Gäste endlich die Musik aus.

3. sie (*pl.*) / den ganzen Abend / wild tanzen
_____, waren sie endlich müde.

4. der Gastgeber / einschlafen
_____, gingen die Gäste endlich nach Hause!

4 **Was hatten sie gemacht?** Complete each sentence with an expression from the list.
Use the **Plusquamperfekt**.

einen Unfall haben	lange in der Schlange warten	noch viele Postkarten schreiben
seine Fahrkarte entwerten	tanken	~~Hausaufgaben machen~~

Beispiel

Bevor ich ins Bett ging, hatte ich Hausaufgaben gemacht.

1. Bevor wir in den Bus einstiegen, _____.
2. Bevor Simon mit der U-Bahn fuhr, _____.
3. Bevor meine Eltern die Polizei anriefen, _____.
4. Bevor ihr gestern nach Stuttgart fuhrt, _____.
5. Bevor du von deiner Reise zurückkamst, _____.

5 **So ein Pech** Emma is always a little late. Write sentences using **als**.

Beispiel

Emma / endlich / zum Flughafen / kommen // das Flugzeug / schon / abfliegen
Als Emma endlich zum Flughafen kam, war das Flugzeug schon abgeflogen.

1. die Polizei / endlich / bei Emma / ankommen // jemand / das Auto / schon / stehlen
_____

2. sie / endlich / zum Bahnhof / kommen // ihr Freund / schon / ein Taxi / nehmen
_____

3. ihr Flugzeug / endlich / landen // der Bus / zum Hotel / schon / abfahren
_____

4. sie / ihren Koffer / endlich packen // ihre Freundin / schon 20 Minuten / warten
_____

4A.2 Comparatives and superlatives

1 **Grundform, Komparativ oder Superlativ?** Indicate whether each sentence uses the **Grundform**, **Komparativ**, or **Superlativ**.

	Grundform	Komparativ	Superlativ
1. Fährt der Zug genauso schnell wie der Bus?	○	○	○
2. Die U-Bahn fährt nachts am schnellsten.	○	○	○
3. Flugzeuge sind die interessantesten Verkehrsmittel.	○	○	○
4. Eine Fahrt mit dem Bus ist teurer als eine Fahrt mit der U-Bahn.	○	○	○
5. Meine Schwester reist lieber mit der Bahn als mit dem Auto.	○	○	○
6. Gibt es genauso viele Autos wie Busse in den USA?	○	○	○
7. Manche Boote kosten mehr als ein kleines Flugzeug.	○	○	○
8. Fahrrad fahren ist am gesündesten.	○	○	○

2 **Was meinen Sie?** Use the elements to write sentences using comparatives of equality: either **genauso...wie** or **so...wie**.

> **Beispiel**
> Ein Jaguar kostet <u>so viel wie ein guter Mercedes</u>.

bequem	langweilig
dumm	schlecht
gern	teuer
interessant	~~viel~~

das Benzin in München
mit dem Bus
~~ein guter Mercedes~~
lange in einer Schlange zu warten

U-Bahnen
ein kaputter Scheibenwischer
der Verkehr in Frankfurt
eine Zugfahrt

1. Ich fahre mit dem Auto _____.
2. Meine Eltern finden Züge _____.
3. Eine Busfahrt ist _____.
4. Der Verkehr in Hamburg ist _____.
5. Das Benzin in Berlin ist _____.
6. Zwölf Stunden mit dem Flugzeug zu fliegen ist _____.
7. Einen Platten zu haben ist _____.

3 **Wie ist es wirklich?** Write sentences using the comparative.

> **Beispiel**
> ein Fluss / sein / lang / eine Straße
> Ein Fluss ist länger als eine Straße.

1. ein Flugzeug / sein / schnell / ein Zug

   _____

2. der Winter / sein / kalt / der Sommer

   _____

3. Schokolade / schmecken / gut / Brokkoli

   _____

4. eine Taxifahrt / kosten / viel / eine Busfahrkarte

   _____

Workbook

4 **Wo ist es am schönsten?** Paula is answering Julius's questions about Bavaria. Complete the dialogue with the correct superlative forms of the appropriate adjectives.

> **Beispiel**
>
> **JULIUS** Wo fahren die <u>pünktlichsten</u> Züge?
> **PAULA** Die Züge in Bayern sind <u>am pünktlichsten</u>.

| freundlich | hoch | ~~pünktlich~~ |
| gut | lang | viel |

JULIUS Wo steht der (1) _____ chinesische Turm?

PAULA Der chinesische Turm in München ist natürlich (2) _____.

JULIUS Wie heißt der (3) _____ Fluss?

PAULA Die Donau ist (4) _____.

JULIUS Wo gibt es die (5) _____ Brötchen?

PAULA Die Brötchen in Bayern heißen Semmeln und schmecken (6) _____.

JULIUS Wer trinkt das (7) _____ Wasser?

PAULA Die Bayern trinken (8) _____.

JULIUS Wo ist der (9) _____ Flughafen?

PAULA Der Flughafen in München ist (10) _____.

5 **Zug oder Flugzeug?** List some advantages (**Vorteile**) and disadvantages (**Nachteile**) of each of the means of transportation depicted. Then write six complete sentences comparing the two.

Vorteile	**Nachteile**		**Vorteile**	**Nachteile**
_____	_____		_____	_____
_____	_____		_____	_____
_____	_____		_____	_____

1. _____

2. _____

3. _____

4. _____

5. _____

6. _____

Workbook

Kapitel 4

Lektion 4B

KONTEXT

1 **Was ist richtig?** Choose the expression that best completes each sentence.

1. Zum Fernsehen braucht man _____.
   a. die Fernbedienung
   b. das Ladegerät
   c. die Tastatur

2. Um eine E-Mail zu schreiben, braucht man _____.
   a. die CD
   b. die DVD
   c. den Laptop

3. Um SMS zu schreiben, benutze ich _____.
   a. die Digitalkamera
   b. das Smartphone
   c. das Passwort

4. Um ein Dokument zu drucken, brauche ich _____.
   a. den Drucker
   b. den Kopfhörer
   c. das Mikrofon

5. Zum Telefonieren benutzt man _____.
   a. das Handy
   b. die Datei
   c. die Kamera

6. Um Musik zu hören, brauche ich _____.
   a. die Website
   b. die Kopfhörer
   c. die Spielkonsole

2 **Was fehlt?** Complete the text with words from the list. Use each word only once.

ausgemacht	geladen
Datei	Ladegerät
Dokument	Laptop
gedruckt	

Jana hat eine (1) _____ auf der Festplatte gespeichert, ein (2) _____ mit einem Drucker (3) _____ und ihren Computer dann (4) _____. Mit einem (5) _____ hat sie ihr Smartphone (6) _____ und dann ein neues Buch auf ihren (7) _____ heruntergeladen.

3 **Was ist das?** Label the parts of the computer and peripherals. Include the definite articles.

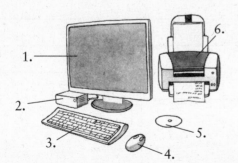

1. _____
2. _____
3. _____
4. _____
5. _____
6. _____

4 **Und heute?** Read the statements about how older generations used technology and rewrite each sentence stating how it's done today.

> eine Fernbedienung benutzen   mit Spielkonsolen spielen
>
> im Internet surfen   E-Mails schreiben
>
> DVDs haben   SMS schicken
>
> ein Smartphone haben   ~~CDs hören~~

Beispiel

Mein alter Lehrer hat noch Kassetten gehört.
Heute hören wir CDs.

1. Meine Eltern haben noch Briefe geschrieben.

   _____

2. Meine Oma ruft mich noch an, wenn sie mich treffen will.

   _____

3. Mein Opa hatte noch Videokassetten.

   _____

4. In den 90er Jahren las man am Morgen beim Frühstück noch die Zeitung.

   _____

5. Früher brauchte man noch eine Kamera, ein Telefon und einen Computer.

   _____

6. Früher musste man noch aufstehen, um das Fernsehprogramm zu ändern.

   _____

7. Meine Eltern spielten noch Tischtennis und Monopoly.

   _____

5 **Und Sie?** What electronics do you own? Write a paragraph describing at least five items.

_____

_____

_____

_____

_____

_____

_____

_____

Workbook

STRUKTUREN

4B.1 The genitive case

1 **Finden Sie den Genitiv** Mark the genitive construction in each sentence.

1. Die neuen Kopfhörer des Vaters sind am besten.
2. Die Website der Universität lädt immer sehr schnell.
3. Gestern hat die Fernbedienung des Fernsehers nicht funktioniert.
4. Wie findest du die Website des Bundespräsidenten?
5. Leider habe ich das Passwort des Computers vergessen.
6. Sein Onkel hat die coolste Spielkonsole der Stadt!
7. Die Technik eines Smartphones ist sehr kompliziert.
8. Nach acht Jahren habe ich die SMS meiner Exfreundin endlich gelöscht!

2 **Was passt?** Indicate the correct genitive preposition.

1. Ich besuche meine Großeltern (während / anstatt) der Woche.
2. (Trotz / Statt) des schlechten Wetters gehen wir im Park spazieren.
3. Die Polizei fand das gestohlene Auto (außerhalb / während) der Stadt.
4. Mein Freund hat einen Laptop (wegen / statt) eines Computers gekauft.
5. (Wegen / Trotz) des teuren Preises kaufe ich mir eine Spielkonsole.
6. Bitte beantworten Sie die E-Mail (wegen / innerhalb) eines Tages.

3 **Schreiben** Rewrite the expressions using the genitive case.

> **Beispiel**
> der kleine Computer: *des kleinen Computers*

1. die alte Tastatur: _____
2. ein neuer Bildschirm: _____
3. ein kluger Bundespräsident: _____
4. eure interessante DVD: _____
5. ihr langweiliger Sender: _____
6. ein langes Dokument: _____
7. mein kompliziertes Passwort: _____
8. meine schnelle Maus: _____

Workbook

4 **Antworten** Answer each question using the **Genitiv**.

Beispiel

—Findest du die Eltern von meiner Freundin nett?
—Ja, ich finde die Eltern deiner Freundin nett.

1. Kennst du das neue Buch von diesem Autor?

   _____

2. Gefällt dir die Farbe von meinem neuen Kleid?

   _____

3. Magst du das Design von dem neuen Smartphone?

   _____

4. Glaubst du der Geschichte von Jasmin?

   _____

5 **Wem gehört was?** Write a sentence for each picture, stating who owns each item.

Beispiel

Das sind die Kopfhörer meines Bruders.

1. dein Onkel   2. eure Cousine   3. unsere Tanten

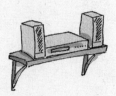

4. sein Opa   5. ihre Schwiegermutter   6. meine Schwestern

1. _____

2. _____

3. _____

4. _____

5. _____

6. _____

4B.2 Demonstratives

1 **Was ist richtig?** Decide which word fits the sentence.

1. (Welchen / Manchen) Laptop kaufst du dir als nächstes?

2. Auf (solche / solchen) Tastaturen tippt man besonders gut.

3. (Jeder / Jedes) gute Passwort sollte mindestens fünf Buchstaben und drei Zahlen haben.

4. Ich arbeite mit (dieser / diesen) neuen Technik nicht gern!

5. (Manches / Manche) Drucker können auch fotokopieren und scannen.

6. (Welche / Welchen) Festplatten speichern heute weniger als zwei GB?

7. Wo ist mein Handy? Ich brauche (das / den) sofort.

8. Die Festplatten (mancher / manche) Menschen sind katastrophal.

2 **Was passt zusammen?** Match the questions on the left with the responses on the right.

1. _____ Ich trinke gern frischen Orangensaft.

2. _____ Gehst du gern zu deinen Nachbarn?

3. _____ Kaufst du gern die CDs von Michael Bublé?

4. _____ Wie schmeckt dir das Brot meiner Mutter?

5. _____ Schläfst du am Wochenende oft lange?

6. _____ Wie findest du den Autor Horst Evers?

a. Ach, der langweilt mich.

b. Ich finde deren Brot immer gut.

c. Igitt. Den trinke ich nicht gern.

d. Leider mache ich das sehr selten.

e. Niemals. Dessen Musik finde ich unmöglich.

f. Oh nein! Bei denen ist es immer so langweilig.

3 **Sätze ergänzen** Complete each sentence with the cues given. Make sure to add the correct ending on the demonstrative as well as the adjective.

> **Beispiel**
>
> _____ Festplatten sind extrem schnell. (dies- / neu)
> **Diese neuen** Festplatten sind extrem schnell.

1. Heute kauft niemand mehr _____ (dies- / alt) Computer.

2. _____ (Jed- / teuer) Digitalkamera macht wunderbare Fotos.

3. Weißt du, _____ (welch- / groß) Bildschirm die beste Qualität hat?

4. Ich will nicht _____ (solch- / langweilig) E-Mails lesen.

5. So _____ (manch- / gut) Programm im Fernsehen kommt erst spät am Abend.

6. Ich kaufe nie wieder _____ (so ein- / langsam) Spielkonsole.

Workbook

Workbook

4 **Was fehlt?** Complete the sentences with either **so ein** or **solcher**. Don't forget to add the appropriate ending.

1. _____ Handy kann man in Europa nicht benutzen.

2. _____ schweren Computer sind nicht mehr auf dem Markt.

3. Mit _____ alten Videokamera kann ich keinen Film machen.

4. _____ dummen E-Mails löscht man am besten sofort.

5 **Schreiben** Describe what the people in the pictures are doing and how often. Use demonstrative pronouns to describe how often.

> **Beispiel**
>
> Frau Arslan kauft jede Woche solche interessanten Bücher.

Frau Arslan

1. Paul und Antonia 2. Lina 3. Ben und Lara 4. die Familie Wagner

1. _____

2. _____

3. _____

4. _____

6 **Werbung!** Create a three-sentence ad for each picture using adjectives and demonstratives. Pay attention to all endings. Use your imagination.

> **Beispiel**
>
> Dieser schnelle Computer hat alles! Nicht mit jedem Computer kann man so schnell im Internet surfen wie mit diesem. Auch das stundenlange Chatten macht manchen Menschen doppelt so viel Spaß! Den müssen Sie kaufen!

1. 2.

1. _____

_____

2. _____

Kapitel 1 — Lektion 1A

KONTEXT

1 **Was passt?** Mark the chart with an **X** for the events the people are celebrating.

	Geburt	Geburtstag	Hochzeit	Rente	Silvester	Weihnachten
1. die Frischvermählten	____	____	____	____	____	____
2. Frau Arslan	____	____	____	____	____	____
3. Wolfgang	____	____	____	____	____	____
4. Kiara	____	____	____	____	____	____
5. die Eltern	____	____	____	____	____	____
6. Baby Emma	____	____	____	____	____	____

2 **Sprechen** Today is Peter's birthday. Look at the pictures and answer the questions you hear. Repeat the correct response after the speaker. (*7 items*)

3 **Antworten** Listen to the story and answer the questions.

Beispiel

You see: Was sind Sabine und Nina?
You hear: Sabine und Nina sind Schwestern.
You write: Sie sind Schwestern.

1. Was planen die Schwestern? _____

2. Wann ist die Party? _____

3. Was muss Sabine schnell machen? _____

4. Wer ist die Gastgeberin? _____

5. Außer Cola, welche Getränke will Nina kaufen? _____

6. Was sollen alle Gäste haben? _____

Lab Manual

AUSSPRACHE UND RECHTSCHREIBUNG

The consonantal *r*

To pronounce the German consonant **r**, start by placing the tip of your tongue against your lower front teeth. Then raise the back of your tongue toward the roof of your mouth. Let air flow from the back of your throat over your tongue creating a soft vibrating sound from the roof of your mouth.

Rock   rot   Brille   Freund   Jahrestag

Note that the consonant **r** sound always precedes a vowel.

Orange   frisch   fahren   Rucksack   Paprika

When the German **r** comes at the end of a word or a syllable, it sounds more like a vowel than a consonant.

---

1 **Aussprechen** Wiederholen Sie die Wörter, die Sie hören.

1. Rente
2. rosa
3. reden
4. Schrank
5. schreiben
6. sprechen
7. Sprudel
8. Straße
9. gestreift
10. frisch
11. Bruder
12. tragen
13. grau
14. Haare
15. Amerika
16. studieren

---

2 **Nachsprechen** Wiederholen Sie die Sätze, die Sie hören.

1. Veronika trägt einen roten Rock.
2. Mein Bruder schreibt einen Brief.
3. Rolf reist mit Rucksack nach Rosenheim.
4. Regensburg und Bayreuth liegen in Bayern.
5. Warum fahren Sie nicht am Freitag?
6. Marie und Robert sprechen Russisch.
7. Drei Krokodile fressen frische Frösche.
8. Im Restaurant bestellt die Frau Roggenbrot mit Radieschen.

---

3 **Sprichwörter** Wiederholen Sie die Sprichwörter, die Sie hören.

1. Rede, so lernst du reden.
2. Der Krug geht so lange zum Brunnen, bis er bricht.

---

4 **Diktat** You will hear six sentences. Each will be read twice. Listen carefully and write what you hear.

1. _____
2. _____
3. _____
4. _____
5. _____
6. _____

Lab Manual

STRUKTUREN

1A.1 The *Perfekt* (Part 1)

1 **Was haben Sie gemacht?** Listen to each sentence and indicate whether the verb is in the present tense or the **Perfekt**.

	Present	*Perfekt*
1.	○	○
2.	○	○
3.	○	○
4.	○	○
5.	○	○
6.	○	○
7.	○	○
8.	○	○

2 **Üben Sie** Change the sentences you hear from the present to the **Perfekt**. Repeat the correct response after the speaker. (*6 items*)

> **Beispiel**
>
> *You hear:* Ich finde die Geburtstagsballons.
> *You say:* Ich habe die Geburtstagsballons gefunden.

3 **Sätze bilden** Build sentences in the **Perfekt** using the cues you hear.

> **Beispiel**
>
> *You see:* Ich _____.
> *You hear:* das Auto / gestern / waschen
> *You write:* Ich *habe gestern das Auto gewaschen.*

1. Ich _____.

2. Der Kellner _____.

3. Die Familie _____.

4. Du _____.

5. Die Restaurantköchin _____.

6. Nina und Paul _____.

7. Der Gastgeber _____.

8. Ihr _____.

Lab Manual

1A.2 Accusative pronouns

1 **Was passt?** Listen and indicate the accusative pronoun you hear.

> **Beispiel**
>
> *You hear:* Opa und Oma Hartmann sind nett. Wir mögen sie.
> *You see:* sie / ihn
> *You mark:* sie

1. euch / mich

2. dich / Sie

3. Sie / sie

4. dich / euch

5. es / ihn

6. sie / uns

2 **Anders gesagt** Listen and rephrase each sentence using an accusative pronoun. Repeat the correct response after the speaker. (*6 items*)

> **Beispiel**
>
> *You hear:* Diese Party ist für Frank.
> *You say:* Diese Party ist für ihn.

3 **Antworten** Answer the questions you hear using accusative pronouns.

1. Ja, sie mag _____ sehr.

2. Ja, sie macht _____ täglich.

3. Ja, sie mögen _____.

4. Nein, sie möchten _____ nicht bestellen.

5. Nein, er braucht _____ nicht.

6. Ja, er möchte _____ haben.

1A.3 Dative pronouns

1 **Was passt?** Identify the dative pronoun that correctly replaces the dative object in the sentences you hear.

> **Beispiel**
>
> *You hear:* Mutters neue Teller gefallen dir und mir.
> *You see:* a. euch
>   b. uns
> *You choose:* b. uns

1. a. ihm   b. ihr

2. a. euch   b. ihnen

3. a. euch   b. uns

4. a. sie   b. ihr

5. a. Ihnen   b. ihr

6. a. euch   b. sie

2 **Sagen Sie es noch einmal** Restate the sentence you hear using a dative pronoun. Repeat the correct response after the speaker. (*6 items*)

> **Beispiel**
>
> *You hear:* Anne dankt Peter für das Geschenk.
> *You say:* Anne dankt ihm für das Geschenk.

3 **Antworten** Answer the questions about the pictures using dative pronouns. There are two questions for each picture. Repeat the correct response after the speaker.

1. Ja, ...   3. Ja, ...   5. Ja, ...   7. Nein, ...

2. Ja, ...   4. Ja, ...   6. Nein, ...   8. Ja, ...

Lab Manual

Kapitel 1   Lektion 1B

KONTEXT

Lab Manual

1 **Wer will was?** Listen to Lina and Holger talk about clothing. Then indicate whether the statements are **richtig** or **falsch**.

	richtig	falsch
1. Lina braucht zwei Röcke.	○	○
2. Lina möchte eine weite Jeans.	○	○
3. Lina will Turnschuhe kaufen.	○	○
4. Holger möchte einen gestreiften Pullover.	○	○
5. Holger zieht blaue Socken an.	○	○
6. Holger will ein Sweatshirt und eine rote Mütze kaufen.	○	○

2 **Wem gefällt was?** Greta and her mother are shopping for a trip to Italy. Listen to what they say and answer the questions. Repeat the correct responses after the speaker.

> **Beispiel**
> *You hear:* Wie findest du das dunkle Kleid?
> *You see:* Ist das Kleid hell oder dunkel?
> *You say:* Das Kleid ist dunkel.

1. Ist die Seidenbluse einfarbig oder gestreift?
2. Ist der Baumwollpullover braun oder rosa?
3. Welche Farbe hat der Hut?
4. Soll der Badeanzug grün oder rot sein?
5. Ist das T-Shirt langärmlig oder kurzärmlig?
6. Ist die Sonnenbrille günstig oder teuer?

3 **Im Geschäft** Answer the questions about each photo. Repeat the correct response after the speaker. (*5 items*).

> **Beispiel**
> *You hear:* Ist das erste Foto ein Geschäft für Frauen?
> *You say:* Nein, das erste Foto ist ein Geschäft für Männer.

AUSSPRACHE UND RECHTSCHREIBUNG

The letter combination *ch* (Part 1)

The letter combination **ch** has two distinct pronunciations, which depend on its placement within a word. To pronounce the **ch** after the vowels **a**, **o**, **u**, and **au**, start by pressing the tip of your tongue against your lower front teeth and raising the back of the tongue to the roof of the mouth. Then blow out air through the small space between the back of the tongue and the roof of the mouth.

    Nachname   Tochter   Buch   brauchen   acht

In loanwords, **ch** may appear at the beginning of a word. In these words, the **ch** is sometimes pronounced like the *k* in the English word *king*. It may also be pronounced like the *sh* in the English word *ship*.

    Chaos   Chor   Christ   Chance   Chef

1   **Aussprechen** Wiederholen Sie die Wörter, die Sie hören.

1. lachen	4. gesprochen	7. fluchen
2. nach	5. geflochten	8. Tuch
3. auch	6. brauchen	9. flache

2   **Nachsprechen** Wiederholen Sie die Sätze, die Sie hören.

1. Wir haben schon wieder Krach mit den Nachbarn.
2. Christians Tochter macht die Nachspeise.
3. Die Kinder waren nass bis auf die Knochen.
4. Hast du Bauchweh?
5. Der Schüler sucht ein Buch über Fremdsprachen.
6. Jochen kocht eine Suppe mit Lauch.

3   **Sprichwörter** Wiederholen Sie die Sprichwörter, die Sie hören.

1. Wo Rauch ist, da ist auch Feuer.
2. Vorgetan und nachgedacht hat manchem großes Leid gebracht.

4   **Diktat** You will hear six sentences. Each will be read twice. Listen carefully and write what you hear.

1. _____
2. _____
3. _____
4. _____
5. _____
6. _____

Lab Manual

STRUKTUREN

1B.1 The *Perfekt* (Part 2)

1

Eine Reise nach Italien Listen to each sentence and indicate whether the verb is in the present tense or the **Perfekt**.

	Present	*Perfekt*
1.	○	○
2.	○	○
3.	○	○
4.	○	○
5.	○	○
6.	○	○
7.	○	○
8.	○	○
9.	○	○
10.	○	○

2

Im Perfekt, bitte Listen and restate each sentence in the **Perfekt**. Repeat the correct response after the speaker. (*7 items*)

> **Beispiel**
>
> *You hear:* Dilara reist nach Leipzig.
> *You say:* Dilara ist nach Leipzig gereist.

3

Sprechen Create sentences in the **Perfekt** combing the subject pronouns you see with the verb phrases you hear. Repeat the correct response after the speaker.

> **Beispiel**
>
> *You hear:* zwei Brötchen essen
> *You see:* ich
> *You say:* Ich habe zwei Brötchen gegessen.

1. wir

2. sie (*sing.*)

3. ich

4. ihr

5. sie (*pl.*)

6. du / ?

7. was / ?

8. Sie (*form., sg.*) / ?

1B.2 *Wissen* and *kennen*

1 **Wissen Sie es?** Listen and restate each sentence using the subject provided. Repeat the correct response after the speaker.

1. Annes Eltern

2. ihr

3. mein Bruder

4. Thomas

5. ich

6. Maria und Lara

7. Frau Neumann

8. du und Anna

2 **Sprechen** Rewrite each sentence you hear using the **Perfekt**. (*6 items*)

> **Beispiel**
>
> *You hear:* Ich weiß deine Adresse nicht.
> *You write:* Ich habe deine Adresse nicht gewusst.

1. _____

2. _____

3. _____

4. _____

5. _____

6. _____

3 **Kennen oder *wissen*?** Create sentences in the present tense combining the subject pronouns you see, the phrases you hear, and the appropriate form of **wissen** or **kennen**. Repeat the correct response after the speaker.

> **Beispiel**
>
> *You see:* ihr / ?
> *You hear:* die Telefonnummer
> *You say:* Wisst ihr die Telefonnummer?

1. ich

2. wir

3. Sie (*form.*) / ?

4. du / ?

5. ihr / ?

6. sie (*pl.*)

7. du / ?

8. er

1B.3 Two-way prepositions

1 **Was fehlt?** Listen to the conversation and fill in the missing prepositions. Then listen again to check your answers.

HASAN Hallo Simon, wohin gehst du?

SIMON Ich gehe (1) _____ die Sporthalle. Unser Team trainiert
(2) _____ den Seminaren.

HASAN Ihr wollt wirklich (3) _____ Platz Eins? Ich kaufe
(4) _____ dem Spiel (5) _____ der Sporthalle ein Ticket.
Ich will (6) _____ Renate sitzen. Unsere Freunde können
(7) _____ uns sitzen.

2 **Sprechen** Complete the sentences using the preposition you hear with the correct accusative or dative form of the definite article. Use contractions where appropriate.

> **Beispiel**
>
> *You see:* Du sitzt _____.
> *You hear:* in
> *You write:* Du sitzt __im__ Zug.

1. Die Freundinnen gehen _____ Geschäft.
2. Die Rechtsanwältin sitzt _____ Schreibtisch.
3. Ihre Papiere liegen _____ Tisch.
4. Sie laufen jeden Morgen _____ Park.
5. Drei schöne T-Shirts sind _____ Bett gefallen.
6. Das Fischgeschäft liegt _____ zwei Bäckereien.
7. Irene stellt die Teller _____ Torte.
8. Der Verkäufer legt die Pullover _____ Rock.
9. Lisa trifft ihre Freundin _____ Mensa.
10. Der Tennisball fliegt _____ Spielfeld.

3 **Wo und wohin** Answer each question you hear with a two-way preposition and the accusative or dative case, as appropriate. Then, repeat the correct response after the speaker.

> **Beispiel**
>
> *You hear:* Wohin gehen Marthas Cousinen gern?
> *You see:* der Wald
> *You say:* Marthas Cousinen gehen gern in den Wald.

1. unter / der Tisch
2. in / die Wäsche
3. vor / die Tafel
4. in / das Restaurant
5. hinter / die guten Studenten
6. an / die Tür
7. in / das Wasser
8. auf / der Schreibtisch

Kapitel 2

Lektion 2A

KONTEXT

1   **Wo machen sie was?** Listen to the conversation and indicate where each activity takes place.

1. Alexandra und Matthias frühstücken _____.	im Esszimmer	in der Küche
2. Matthias arbeitet _____.	im Wohnzimmer	im Arbeitszimmer
3. Alexandra wäscht den Hund _____.	im Badezimmer	im Keller
4. Das neue Sofa kommt _____.	ins Schlafzimmer	ins Wohnzimmer
5. Der Nachttisch muss _____.	auf den Dachboden	in den Keller
6. Sie stellen die Kommode _____.	ins Schlafzimmer	auf den Dachboden

2   **Die Wohnung** Answer the questions you hear using the locations you see. Repeat the correct response after the speaker.

> **Beispiel**
>
> *You hear:* Jutta arbeitet nicht im Schlafzimmer. Wo arbeitet sie?
> *You see:* im Arbeitszimmer
> *You say:* Sie arbeitet im Arbeitszimmer.

1. im Sessel
2. im Bett im Schlafzimmer
3. in der Küche

4. im Keller
5. im Badezimmer
6. an der Wand

3   **Beschreiben Sie** Answer the questions about the picture in complete sentences.

1. _____
2. _____
3. _____
4. _____
5. _____

Lab Manual

AUSSPRACHE UND RECHTSCHREIBUNG

The letter combination *ch* (Part 2)

To pronounce the soft **ch** after the vowel sounds **i/ie, e, ä, ö, ü,** or **ei,** start by placing the tip of your tongue behind your lower teeth. Then pronounce the *h* sound while breathing out forcefully.

Chemie	rechts	Teppich	Küche	leicht

Use the same soft **ch** sound when pronouncing the **g** in the suffix **-ig** at the end of a word. However, when there is an adjective ending after the **-ig**, the **g** is pronounced like the hard *g* in the word *garden*. In the combination **-iglich**, the **g** is pronounced like the *k* in the word *kind*. The soft **ch** is also used in the suffix **-lich**, whether or not there is an ending after it.

dreckig	schmutzig	billige	königlich	freundlichen

When **ch** appears before an **s**, the letter combination is pronounced like the *x* in the word *fox*. Do not confuse **chs** with the combination **sch**, which is pronounced like the *sh* in the word *shade*.

sechs	wachsen	schlafen	waschen	Dachs

When **ch** appears at the beginning of loanwords, its pronunciation varies.

Charakter	Chip	Chef	Charterflug	Chronik

1 **Aussprechen** Wiederholen Sie die Wörter, die Sie hören.

1. Bücher
2. freundlich
3. China
4. zwanzig
5. braunhaarige
6. lediglich
7. höchste
8. Achsel
9. Ochse
10. Chaos
11. checken
12. Charme

2 **Nachsprechen** Wiederholen Sie die Sätze, die Sie hören.

1. Die königliche Köchin schläft wieder in der Küche.
2. Mein neugieriger Nachbar will täglich mit mir sprechen.
3. Den Rechtsanwalt finden wir freundlich und zuverlässig.
4. Der Chef schickt mich nächstes Jahr nach China.
5. Der Dachs hat einen schlechten Charakter.

3 **Sprichwörter** Wiederholen Sie die Sprichwörter, die Sie hören.

1. Liebe deinen Nächsten wie dich selbst.
2. Jedem Tierchen sein Pläsierchen.

4 **Diktat** You will hear five sentences. Each will be read twice. Listen carefully and write what you hear.

1. _____
2. _____
3. _____
4. _____
5. _____

Lab Manual

STRUKTUREN

2A.1 The *Präteritum*

1 **Was hören Sie?** Listen and indicate the verb form you hear.

1. kochtest	kocht	kochte
2. dürfen	durften	durftet
3. mochte	mögen	möchte
4. schliefen... ein	schliefst... ein	schlief... ein
5. schriebt	schrieb	schrieben
6. waren	warst	wart
7. hatte	haben	hatten
8. überraschtest	überraschen	überraschten

2 **Sprechen** Restate each sentence using the **Präteritum** form of the verb. Repeat the correct response after the speaker. (*6 items*)

> **Beispiel**
> *You hear:* Ich wohne in einer Wohnung.
> *You say:* Ich wohnte in einer Wohnung.

3 **Was machten sie?** Respond to each statement, saying whether the person indicated did the same activity. Repeat the correct response after the speaker.

> **Beispiel**
> *You hear:* Wir gingen angeln.
> *You see:* Tony / nicht
> *You say:* Tony ging nicht angeln.

1. ich
2. wir
3. du / nicht
4. sie (*pl.*) / nicht
5. er
6. Sie (*formal*)
7. ich / nicht
8. ihr / nicht

Lab Manual

2A.2 Da-, wo-, hin-, and her-compounds

1 **Markieren Sie** You will hear eight sentences. Mark **X** under the compounds you hear.

> *Beispiel*
>
> *You hear:* Wohin geht ihr?
> *You mark:* an X under wohin

	daran	dafür	darin	darunter	hinauf	wohin	worauf	wozu
Beispiel						X		
1.								
2.								
3.								
4.								
5.								
6.								
7.								
8.								

2 **Sprechen** You will hear six sentences. Choose the correct follow-up sentence from the list. Say the new sentence and repeat the correct response after the speaker. (*6 items*)

> *Beispiel*
>
> *You hear:* Wir sind im Erdgeschoss.
> *You say:* Wir gehen die Treppe ins fünfte Stockwerk hinauf.

> Bitte wartet davor auf mich, ok?
> Ich habe sie herunter ins Wohnzimmer getragen.
> Ich habe sie vom Garten herauf gebracht.
> Ich danke dir dafür!
> Kannst du sie darunter sehen?
> ~~Wir gehen die Treppe ins fünfte Stockwerk hinauf.~~
> Wohin zieht ihr um, in die Ringstraße?

3 **Wo-Fragen** You will hear six statements. For each one, write a question using a **wo**-compound.

1. _____
2. _____
3. _____
4. _____
5. _____
6. _____

Lab Manual

2A.3 Coordinating conjunctions

1 **Was passt?** Mark **X** under the coordinating conjunction you hear.

	aber	denn	oder	sondern	und
1.	____	____	____	____	____
2.	____	____	____	____	____
3.	____	____	____	____	____
4.	____	____	____	____	____
5.	____	____	____	____	____
6.	____	____	____	____	____
7.	____	____	____	____	____

2 **Sprechen** Combine the clauses you see and those you hear using the appropriate coordinating conjunction. Say the complete sentence aloud. Then, repeat the correct response after the speaker.

> **Beispiel**
>
> *You see:* Die Vase steht nicht unter dem Tisch, _____.
> *You hear:* darauf
> *You say:* Die Vase steht nicht unter dem Tisch, sondern darauf.

1. Willst du das rote Kleid anziehen _____?

2. Der braune Gürtel ist schön, _____.

3. Öffne die Kellertür, bitte, _____.

4. Unsere neue Wohnung ist sehr angenehm _____.

5. Rita wohnt nicht im Erdgeschoss, _____.

3 **Was fehlt?** You will hear six pairs of sentences. Restate each pair of prompts as a single sentence using a coordinating conjunction. Repeat the correct response after the speaker. (*6 items*)

> **Beispiel**
>
> *You hear:* Willst du Brokkoli essen? Willst du Kuchen essen?
> *You say:* Willst du Brokkoli oder Kuchen essen?

Lab Manual

Kapitel 2 Lab Activities

Kapitel 2

KONTEXT

Lektion 2B

1 **Logisch oder unlogisch?** Indicate whether each statement you hear is **logisch** or **unlogisch**.

	logisch	unlogisch
1.	○	○
2.	○	○
3.	○	○
4.	○	○
5.	○	○
6.	○	○
7.	○	○
8.	○	○

2 **Eriks Hausarbeit** Respond to each prompt you hear with a complete sentence about Erik's chores. Repeat the correct response after the speaker. (*6 items*)

Beispiel

You hear: spülen, das schmutzige Geschirr
You say: **Erik spült das schmutzige Geschirr.**

3 **Nach dem Besuch** Birgit's messy friends have gone back home after a short visit. Look at the picture and answer the questions you hear using complete sentences.

1. _____

2. _____

3. _____

4. _____

5. _____

AUSSPRACHE UND RECHTSCHREIBUNG

The German *k*-sound

The German **k** is pronounced like the *k* in the English word *kind*. At the end of a syllable, this sound may be written as a **ck**.

| Kaffee | Laken | Decke | Frack | Kreide |

In a few loanwords, the **c** at the beginning of a word is pronounced like a **k**. In other loanwords, the initial **c** may be pronounced similarly to the *ts* in *cats* or the *c* in *cello*.

| Computer | Caravan | Couch | Celsius | Cello |

When the consonant combination **kn** appears at the beginning of a word, both letters are pronounced. In the combination **nk**, the sound is very similar to the *nk* in the English word *thank*.

| Knie | knusprig | Knödel | danken | Schrank |

Remember that the **ch** sound and the **k/ck** sound are pronounced differently.

| dich | dick | Bach | Back |

---

1   **Aussprechen** Wiederholen Sie die Wörter, die Sie hören.

1. Keller	4. Container	7. knackig	10. Hockey
2. Keramik	5. Cola	8. Knallfrosch	11. lach
3. Stock	6. Celsius	9. Bank	12. Lack

---

2   **Nachsprechen** Wiederholen Sie die Sätze, die Sie hören.

1. In der Küche bäckt man Kekse.
2. Deine Kleider hängen im Kleiderschrank.
3. In Frankfurt essen glückliche Kinder knackige Bockwürste.
4. Mein Lieblingsmöbelstück ist diese knallrote Couch.
5. Wir kaufen das Cabriolet in Köln.
6. Kann Klaus Knödel kochen?

---

3   **Sprichwörter** Wiederholen Sie die Sprichwörter, die Sie hören.

1. Klappern gehört zum Handwerk.
2. Kommt Zeit, kommt Rat.

---

4   **Diktat** You will hear six sentences. Each will be read twice. Listen carefully and write what you hear.

1. _____
2. _____
3. _____
4. _____
5. _____
6. _____

Lab Manual

STRUKTUREN

2B.1 *Perfekt* versus *Präteritum*

1 **Was hören Sie?** Listen and indicate the tense you hear.

	Perfekt	Präteritum	Present		Perfekt	Präteritum	Present
1.	○	○	○	5.	○	○	○
2.	○	○	○	6.	○	○	○
3.	○	○	○	7.	○	○	○
4.	○	○	○	8.	○	○	○

2 **Präteritum oder Perfekt?** You will hear five sentences. Write each verb you hear in the appropriate column. Sometimes, both verbs in a sentence belong in the same column.

> **Beispiel**
>
> *You hear:* Als ich jung war, habe ich keine Hausarbeit gemacht.
> *You write:* war under Präteritum and habe gemacht under Perfekt

	Präteritum	Perfekt
Beispiel	war	habe gemacht
1.		
2.		
3.		
4.		
5.		

3 **Antworten** Answer the questions you hear about each picture. Then repeat the correct response after the speaker.

> **Beispiel**
>
> *You see:* schmutzig sein
> *You hear:* Warum wolltest du die Wäsche waschen?
> *You say:* Ich wollte die Wäsche waschen, denn sie war schmutzig.

schmutzig sein

1. die Waschmaschine nicht verstehen können

2. ihn anrufen

3. mir die Waschmaschine erklären

4. mir helfen

Lab Manual

2B.2 Separable and inseparable prefix verbs in the *Perfekt*

1 **Ordnen Sie die Verben ein** You will hear eight infinitives. Write the 3rd person singular **Perfekt** form in the appropriate column. Include both the auxiliary and the past participle.

Beispiel

> You hear: aufräumen
>
> You write: *hat aufgeräumt* under separable prefix

	separable prefix	inseparable prefix
Beispiel	*hat aufgeräumt*	
1.		
2.		
3.		
4.		
5.		
6.		
7.		
8.		

2 **Antworten** You will hear a question about each picture. Answer each question in the present perfect using the logical verb phrase. Repeat the correct response after the speaker.

Beispiel

> You see: ihr Lieblingsbuch entdecken / die Bücher abstauben
>
> You hear: Was hat die Bibliothekarin gemacht?
>
> You say: *Die Bibliothekarin hat ihr Lieblingsbuch entdeckt.*

1. einen Freund anrufen / einen Freund besuchen

2. die Professorin bezahlen / die Professorin nicht verstehen

3. aus Italien zurückkommen / den Müll hinausbringen

4. ein Café besuchen / eine Blume mitbringen

3 **Im Perfekt, bitte** Rewrite each sentence you hear using the **Perfekt**.

1. _____
2. _____
3. _____
4. _____
5. _____
6. _____
7. _____

Lab Manual

Kapitel 3

KONTEXT

1   **Das Wetter** You will hear eight statements. Write the number of each statement you hear below the picture it describes. There are two statements for each picture.

a. _____ _____

b. _____ _____

c. _____ _____

d. _____ _____

2   **Was passt zusammen?** You will hear six groups of words. For each group, write the word that is unrelated to the others.

> **Beispiel**
>
> *You hear:* der Frühling, der Winter, der Monat
> *You write:*   der Monat

1. _____   4. _____

2. _____   5. _____

3. _____   6. _____

3   **Antworten** You will hear a statement followed by a question. Answer the question with a complete sentence.

> **Beispiel**
>
> *You hear:* So ein Sturm, mit Blitz und Donner! Wie ist das Wetter?
> *You say:* Das Wetter ist schlecht.

AUSSPRACHE UND RECHTSCHREIBUNG

Long and short vowels

German vowels can be either long or short. Long vowels are longer in duration and typically occur before a single consonant, before the letter **h**, or when the vowel is doubled. Short vowels are shorter in duration and usually occur before two consonants.

Meter	mehr	Meer	Messer	melden

The long **a** is pronounced like the *a* in the English word *calm*, but with the mouth wide open. The short **a** sounds almost like the long **a**, but it is held for a shorter period of time and pronounced with the mouth more closed.

mahnen	Mann	lasen	lassen

The long **e** sounds like the *a* in the English word *late*. The short **e** sounds like the *e* in *pet*. The long **i** may be written as **i** or **ie**. It is pronounced like the *e* in *be*. The short **i** is pronounced like the *i* in *mitt*.

wen	wenn	Visum	fliegen	Zimmer

The long **o** is pronounced like the *o* in *hope*, but with the lips firmly rounded. The short **o** is pronounced like the *o* in *moth*, but with the lips rounded. The long **u** is pronounced like the *u* in *tuna*, but with the lips firmly rounded. The short **u** is pronounced like the *u* in *put*, but with the lips rounded.

Zoo	Zoll	Flug	Hund

1 **Aussprechen** Wiederholen Sie die Wörter, die Sie hören.

1. Haken / hacken
2. den / denn
3. Bienen / binnen
4. Sohn / Sonne
5. buchen / Bucht
6. Nase / nass
7. fehl / Fell
8. Miete / Mitte
9. wohne / Wonne
10. Humor / Hummer
11. Wagen / Wangen
12. Zehner / Zentner
13. Linie / Linde
14. Lot / Lotto
15. Mus / muss

2 **Nachsprechen** Wiederholen Sie die Sätze, die Sie hören.

1. Viele machen im Sommer Urlaub am Strand.
2. Wolf und Monika wollen den ganzen Tag in der Sonne liegen.
3. Sabine und Michael schwimmen lieber im Meer.
4. Alle sieben Studenten übernachten in einer Jugendherberge.
5. Hast du den Flug schon gebucht?
6. Wenn das Wetter schlecht ist, gehen wir ins Museum.

3 **Sprichwörter** Wiederholen Sie die Sprichwörter, die Sie hören.

1. Liebe geht durch den Magen.
2. Ende gut, alles gut.

4 **Diktat** You will hear seven sentences. Each will be read twice. Listen carefully and write what you hear.

1. _____
2. _____
3. _____
4. _____
5. _____
6. _____
7. _____

Lab Manual

STRUKTUREN

3A.1 Separable and inseparable prefix verbs (*Präteritum*)

1 **Ordnen Sie die Verben ein** You will hear eight infinitives. Write their **Präteritum** forms in the appropriate columns of the chart.

> **Beispiel**
>
> *You hear:* anrufen
> *You see:* ich
> *You write: ich rief an* under *separable prefix*

		separable prefix	inseparable prefix
Beispiel	ich	*ich rief an*	
1.	wir		
2.	er		
3.	ihr		
4.	du		
5.	sie (pl.)		
6.	ich		
7.	du		
8.	Sie (form.)		

2 **Sprechen** Answer the questions you hear using the **Präteritum** with the information provided.

> **Beispiel**
>
> *You hear:* Was machtest du heute Morgen?
> *You see:* das Zimmer aufräumen
> *You say:* Ich räumte das Zimmer auf.

1. nach 10 Uhr aufstehen
2. ihr Auto verkaufen
3. den Zweiten Weltkrieg besprechen
4. in der Innenstadt einkaufen
5. früh einschlafen
6. mit Freunden ausgehen
7. fernsehen
8. viel Zeit mit seiner Professorin verbringen

3 **Im Präteritum, bitte** Rewrite the sentences you hear using the **Präteritum**.

1. Vor dem Essen _____ .
2. Wir _____ .
3. Ich _____ .
4. Sie _____ .
5. Du _____ .
6. Uwe _____ .
7. _____ ?
8. Matthias _____ .

3A.2 Prepositions of location; Prepositions in set phrases

1 **Standort oder Richtung?** Decide whether the preposition in each sentence you hear refers to a **location** or a **direction**.

	location	direction		location	direction
1.	○	○	5.	○	○
2.	○	○	6.	○	○
3.	○	○	7.	○	○
4.	○	○	8.	○	○

2 **Paulas Zimmer** Answer each question about the picture using the preposition **an**, **auf**, **hinter**, **in**, or **neben** with the location provided. Repeat the correct response after the speaker.

> **Beispiel**
> *You hear:* Wo ist der Fernseher?
> *You see:* die Wand
> *You say:* Der Fernseher ist an der Wand.

1. der Schrank   5. das Bett

2. das Bett   6. Karin

3. die Wand   7. die Decke

4. der Schreibtisch 8. die CDs

3 **Was machen sie?** Write sentences combining the verb expression you hear with the words provided.

> **Beispiel**
> *You hear:* Angst haben vor
> *You see:* Daniel / der Hund _____
> *You write:* Daniel hat Angst vor dem Hund.

1. wir / der Sommer _____

2. die Architektin / der Rechtsanwalt _____

3. Oma und Opa / ihre Hochzeit _____

4. der Meteorologe / das schlechte Wetter _____

5. Inga / unsere Adresse _____

6. Niklas und Nina / Hausarbeit _____

7. ich / meine Freunde _____

Lab Manual

Kapitel 3 Lab Activities |

Kapitel 3 **Lektion 3B**

KONTEXT

---

1   **Bilder beschreiben** For each picture, you will hear two statements. Choose the statement that describes the action shown in the picture.

1. a.   b.   2. a.   b.   3. a.   b.

---

2   **Im Reisebüro** Answer the travel agent's questions using the cues provided.

> **Beispiel**
>
> *You hear:* Wohin möchten Sie reisen?
> *You see:* nach Deutschland
> *You say:* Ich möchte nach Deutschland reisen.

1. in Italien
2. am Strand
3. eine Kreuzfahrt
4. Touristenklasse
5. mit dem Auto
6. eine Jugendherberge
7. für eine Woche
8. ja, schon

---

3   **Was passt nicht?** You will hear eight sets of words. For each set, write the word or phrase that does not belong.

1. _____
2. _____
3. _____
4. _____
5. _____
6. _____
7. _____
8. _____

Lab Manual

AUSSPRACHE UND RECHTSCHREIBUNG

Pure vowels versus diphthongs

German has three diphthongs: **au**, **ai/ei**, and **eu/äu**. In these vowel combinations, two vowel sounds are pronounced together in the same syllable.

Haus	Mai	meine	scheu	läuft

All other German vowel sounds are pure vowels. Whether long or short, they never glide into another vowel sound.

kalt	Schnee	Spiel	Monat	Schule

Be sure to pronounce the vowels in German words as pure vowel sounds, even when they resemble English words with similar pronunciations.

kann	Stereo	Apfel	Boot	Schuh

1   **Aussprechen** Wiederholen Sie die Wörter, die Sie hören.

1. Hagel	5. minus	9. Januar	13. Zeit
2. wann	6. Winter	10. Geburtstag	14. heute
3. Regen	7. Oktober	11. August	15. Häuser
4. Wetter	8. Sommer	12. Mai	16. Gasthaus

2   **Nachsprechen** Wiederholen Sie die Sätze, die Sie hören.

1. Es hat fast den ganzen Tag geregnet.
2. Im Juli ist es am Nachmittag zu heiß.
3. Im Winter gehe ich gern Ski laufen.
4. Trink eine Tasse Tee, damit du wieder wach wirst.
5. Im Mai wird es schön warm und sonnig.
6. Im Sommer schwimmen die Kinder im See.
7. Im Herbst muss Max sein Segelboot reparieren lassen.
8. Meine Freundin besucht mich heute.

3   **Sprichwörter** Wiederholen Sie die Sprichwörter, die Sie hören.

1. Morgen, morgen, nur nicht heute, sagen alle faulen Leute.
2. Nach Regen kommt Sonnenschein.

4   **Diktat** You will hear six sentences. Each will be read twice. Listen carefully and write what you hear.

1. _____
2. _____
3. _____
4. _____
5. _____
6. _____

Lab Manual

STRUKTUREN

3B.1 Infinitive expressions and clauses

1 **Was fehlt?** Complete the sentences with the information you hear.

1. Wir buchen unsere Reise, _____.

2. Es macht Spaß, _____.

3. Wir müssen _____.

4. Der junge Mann hilft mir, _____.

5. Du hast vergessen, _____.

6. _____, müssen wir pünktlich am Schiff sein.

2 **Sätze bilden** Form sentences with the cues you see and the infinitive expressions you hear. Repeat the correct response after the speaker. (6 *items*)

> **Beispiel**
>
> *You see:* Ich habe Lust...
> *You hear:* in Urlaub fahren
> *You say:* Ich habe Lust, in Urlaub zu fahren.

1. Ich habe vergessen,...

2. Es ist nicht einfach,...

3. Es macht keinen Spaß,...

4. Es ist Zeit,...

5. Es ist wichtig,...

6. Jetzt ist es schon zu spät,...

3 **Antworten** Answer each question using the information provided. Repeat the correct response after the speaker.

> **Beispiel**
>
> *You hear:* Haben Sie etwas vergessen?
> *You see:* meinen Personalausweis / mitbringen
> *You say:* Ja, ich habe vergessen, meinen Personalausweis mitzubringen.

1. mir / mit meinem Koffer / helfen

2. um / im Reisebüro mein Hotel / buchen

3. im Hotelschwimmbad / schwimmen

4. um / Ihnen den Zimmerschlüssel / geben

5. keinen Urlaub / machen

6. um / ein Zimmer / bekommen

7. durch die Passkontrolle / kommen

8. nur zwei Monate / warten

Lab Manual

3B.2 Time expressions

1 **Was ist richtig?** For each sentence you hear, mark the logical response.

1. ____ a. War es einfach, das Kino zu finden?
   ____ b. Das war ein langer Film.

2. ____ a. Schwimmt er im Meer?
   ____ b. Am Strand sind viele Touristen.

3. ____ a. Das Flugzeug fliegt am 17. Juli.
   ____ b. Diesmal habe ich es schon vor drei Monaten gekauft.

4. ____ a. Die Kreuzfahrt macht sehr viel Spaß.
   ____ b. Seit Wochen wollten sie neue Kleider für die Reise kaufen.

5. ____ a. Letztes Jahr.
   ____ b. Am Dienstag, dem 21. Juni.

6. ____ a. Du wartest schon so lange auf deine Urlaubsreise.
   ____ b. Ich bekomme keinen Urlaub.

2 **Wie oft?** You will hear six sentences. Restate each sentence adding the appropriate time expression. Repeat the correct response after the speaker.

> **Beispiel**
>
> *You hear:* Gehen Sie angeln?
> *You see:* manchmal / zum letzten Mal
> *You say:* Gehen Sie manchmal angeln?

1. dreimal täglich / sechs Monate
2. manchmal / zum ersten Mal
3. einmal / diesmal

4. zum letzten Mal / einmal
5. zweimal in der Woche / manchmal
6. niemals / zweimal jährlich

3 **Was ist passiert?** You will hear a story about Klara and Erik's first day of vacation. Match the pictures with the sequence of events in the story by writing the adverb **zuerst, dann, danach,** or **zuletzt** under each picture.

a. _____ b. _____ c. _____ d. _____

Lab Manual

3B.3 Indefinite pronouns

1 **Was hören Sie?** Listen to each sentence and mark an **X** under the indefinite pronoun you hear.

	alles	etwas	jemand	man	nichts	niemand
1.	_____	_____	_____	_____	_____	_____
2.	_____	_____	_____	_____	_____	_____
3.	_____	_____	_____	_____	_____	_____
4.	_____	_____	_____	_____	_____	_____
5.	_____	_____	_____	_____	_____	_____
6.	_____	_____	_____	_____	_____	_____

2 **Das ist unklar** Restate each sentence you hear using the indefinite pronoun provided. Add any necessary case endings. Repeat the correct response after the speaker.

> **Beispiel**
>
> *You hear:* Ich habe Stefan von meinem Urlaub erzählt.
> *You see:* niemand
> *You say:* Ich habe niemandem von meinem Urlaub erzählt.

1. alles

2. jemand

3. etwas

4. man

5. alles

6. jemand

3 **Was fehlt?** Based on the information you hear, complete each sentence with the appropriate indefinite pronoun: **alle, etwas, jemand, man, nichts**, or **niemand**. Add the appropriate case endings as needed.

> **Beispiel**
>
> *You hear:* Alle blieben lange auf der Party.
> *You see:* _____ ging früh nach Hause.
> *You write:* ___Niemand___ ging früh nach Hause.

1. _____ steht vor der Tür und möchte sie besuchen.

2. _____ hilft ihnen.

3. Er isst zweimal von _____ auf dem Tisch.

4. Sie hat heute noch _____ gegessen.

5. Gib mir bitte _____ davon.

6. _____ feiert jeden Tag eine große Party.

Kapitel 4

Lektion 4A

KONTEXT

1 **Logisch oder unlogisch?** Listen to each statement and indicate whether it is **logisch** or **unlogisch**.

	logisch	unlogisch
1.	○	○
2.	○	○
3.	○	○
4.	○	○
5.	○	○
6.	○	○
7.	○	○
8.	○	○

Beispiel

You hear: Das Fahrrad braucht Benzin.
You mark: unlogisch

2 **Frage und Antwort** Jan has seen an ad for a used car and is calling the owner to get more information. Match each of his questions with the appropriate answer.

Beispiel

You hear: 1. Wie alt ist das Auto?
You see: a. Sechs Jahre alt.
You write: the number 1 next to the letter a

_____ a. Sechs Jahre alt.

_____ b. Es ist rot.

_____ c. 9.500 Euro.

_____ d. So um die 22 Liter.

_____ e. Einen V6.

_____ f. Vier Türen.

_____ g. Eigentlich sehr groß, etwa zwei Quadratmeter.

3 **Antworten** Answer the questions you hear using expressions from the list in the correct case and with the correct verb form. Repeat the correct response after the speaker. (*5 items*)

Beispiel

You hear: Wo wartet der Student?
You see: die Bushaltestelle
You say: Der Student wartet an der Bushaltestelle.

die Bremsen reparieren	ein Bußgeld	rechts abbiegen
~~die Bushaltestelle~~	die Fahrkarten entwerten	die Tankstelle

Lab Manual

AUSSPRACHE UND RECHTSCHREIBUNG

Long and short vowels with an *Umlaut*

You have already learned that adding an **Umlaut** to the vowels **a**, **o**, and **u** changes their pronunciation. Vowels with an **Umlaut** have both long and short forms.

Räder   **Männer**   **löhnen**   **löschen**   **Züge**   **fünf**

The long **ä** is pronounced similarly to the *a* in the English word *bay*, without the final *y* sound. The short **ä** is pronounced like the *e* in *pet*.

Faxgerät   **Unterwäsche**   **Fahrpläne**   **Spaziergänge**

To produce the long **ö** sound, start by saying the German long **e**, but round your lips as if you were about to whistle. To produce the short **ö** sound, start by saying the short **e**, but keep your lips rounded.

Öl   **öffentlich**   **schön**   **Töchter**

To produce the long **ü** sound, start by saying the German long **i**, but round your lips tightly. To produce the short **ü** sound, make the short **i** sound, but with tightly rounded lips. In some loanwords, the German **y** is pronounced like the **ü**. In other loanwords, the German **y** is pronounced like the English consonant *y*.

Schüler   **zurück**   **Typ**   **Physik**

1 **Aussprechen** Wiederholen Sie die Wörter, die Sie hören.

1. Rad / Räder
2. Kopf / Köpfe
3. Zug / Züge
4. Käse / Kästchen
5. mögen / möchten
6. fühlen / füllen
7. kämen / kämmen
8. lösen / löschen
9. Dünen / dünn
10. typisch
11. MP3-Player
12. Handy

2 **Nachsprechen** Wiederholen Sie die Sätze, die Sie hören.

1. In der Küche kocht die Köchin mit einem großen Kochlöffel.
2. Sie ändern morgen alle Fahrpläne für die Züge in Österreich.
3. Lösch alles auf der Festplatte, bevor du deinen PC verkaufst.
4. Jürgen fährt mit öffentlichen Verkehrsmitteln zur Universität.
5. Grüne Fahrräder sind schöner als rote oder schwarze Fahrräder.
6. Der blonde Typ da hat sein Handy verloren.

3 **Sprichwörter** Wiederholen Sie die Sprichwörter, die Sie hören.

1. Ein goldener Schlüssel öffnet alle Türen.
2. Der Apfel fällt nicht weit vom Stamm.

4 **Diktat** You will hear five sentences. Each will be read twice. Listen carefully and write what you hear.

1. _____
2. _____
3. _____
4. _____
5. _____

Lab Manual

STRUKTUREN

4A.1 *Das Plusquamperfekt*

1 *Plusquamperfekt* **oder** *Präteritum?* Write the two verbs you hear in each sentence in the column for the corresponding tense.

Beispiel

You hear: Als ich das dritte Stück Pizza nahm, hatte ich schon genug (*enough*) gegessen.
You write: nahm under *Präteritum,* and *hatte gegessen* under *Plusquamperfekt*

	Präteritum	Plusquamperfekt
Beispiel	*nahm*	*hatte gegessen*
1.	_____	_____
2.	_____	_____
3.	_____	_____

	Präteritum	Plusquamperfekt
4.	_____	_____
5.	_____	_____
6.	_____	_____

2 **Sprechen** Change each sentence you hear from the **Perfekt** to the **Plusquamperfekt**. Repeat the correct answer after the speaker. (6 *items*)

Beispiel

You hear: Ich bin in die Schule gegangen.
You say: Ich war in die Schule gegangen.

3 **Was fehlt?** Complete the sentences with the **Plusquamperfekt** form of the verb you hear.

1. Nachdem Tina im Urlaub _____ _____, zeigte sie ihren Freunden die Fotos.
2. Als sie Tinas Fotos anschauten, _____ die Freunde schon von ihrer nächsten Reise _____.

3. Bevor Frank zur Arbeit ging, _____ er in der Bäckerei _____.
4. Nachdem Frank ein schönes Brötchen _____ _____, verkaufte ihm Ina auch ein Brot.

5. Nachdem der Kaffee schon kalt war, _____ alle noch bei der Arbeit _____.
6. Nachdem sie lang am Computer _____ _____, war Martina sehr müde.

7. Hermanns _____ ihre neue Kleidung _____, bevor sie essen gingen.
8. Hermanns waren müde, nachdem sie nach Mitternacht nach Hause _____ _____.

Lab Manual

4A.2 Comparatives and superlatives

1   **Gut, besser, am besten** You will hear nine sentences. Write the comparative or superlative you hear in the appropriate column.

> **Beispiel**
>
> *You hear:* Inas Haar ist länger als Emmas.
> *You write:* *länger* in the *comparative* column

	comparative	superlative
Beispiel	*länger*	_____
1.	_____	_____
2.	_____	_____
3.	_____	_____
4.	_____	_____

	comparative	superlative
5.	_____	_____
6.	_____	_____
7.	_____	_____
8.	_____	_____
9.	_____	_____

2   **Sprechen** You will hear eight statements. Make a comparison based on each statement you hear and the information you see. Repeat the correct response after the speaker.

> **Beispiel**
>
> *You hear:* Ich bin 1,80 Meter groß.
> *You see:* + / Mein Vater
> *You say:* Mein Vater ist größer als ich.

> = *exactly the same as*
> ≠ *not as … as*
> + *more than*

1. + / Beates Freundin
2. + / Manfred
3. + / ich
4. = / Onkel Willi

5. + / das Badezimmer
6. ≠ / der Porsche
7. = / Michaels Haus
8. ≠ / der Hut

3   **Was fehlt?** Complete each statement with the appropriate superlative form based on the information you hear. (*7 items*)

> **Beispiel**
>
> *You hear:* Sebastian liebt seine Katze mehr als seinen Fisch.
> *You see:* Aber er liebt seinen Hund _____.
> *You write:* ____am meisten____

1. Maria ist _____ Schwester.

2. Sie läuft _____.

3. Es ist _____ Kunstmuseum in Deutschland.

4. Aber Tennis spielen wir _____.

5. Aber ich finde, es ist _____, einen Informatikabschluss zu haben.

6. Aber Februar ist _____ Monat.

7. Aber _____ Flughafen zu uns ist Hanau.

Lab Manual

Kapitel 4   Lektion 4B

KONTEXT

1   **Was passt?** Match each word you hear with its function.

1. _____   a. am Computer schreiben
2. _____   b. anmachen und ausmachen
3. _____   c. Programme im Fernsehen zeigen
4. _____   d. eine Notiz mit dem Handy schreiben
5. _____   e. Informationen speichern
6. _____   f. Websites und Dokumente sehen
7. _____   g. auf eine Datei klicken
8. _____   h. Fotos machen

2   **Wer sagt das?** Listen as Sara and Florian compare their new smartphones. Then indicate whether each feature listed applies to Sara's phone, Florian's phone, or both.

Das Smartphone ...	Saras	Florians	Saras und Florians
1. ist silber und extrem dünn.	○	○	○
2. hat unbegrenztes (*unlimited*) Datenvolumen.	○	○	○
3. hat 78 Euro gekostet.	○	○	○
4. hat einen Micro-SD-Slot.	○	○	○
5. hat ein kleineres Display.	○	○	○

3   **Was ist richtig?** Choose the logical answer to each question you hear.

1. _____ a. Sie wollen neue Filme anschauen.
   _____ b. Sie löschen Informationen von einer Datei.

2. _____ a. Sie sieht gern fern.
   _____ b. Sie will beim Sport Musik hören.

3. _____ a. Es hat ein Mikrofon und eine Kamera.
   _____ b. Er will viele SMS schreiben.

4. _____ a. Sie braucht ihn für ihre Arbeit.
   _____ b. Sie startet das Programm.

5. _____ a. Sie hat ein neues Programm heruntergeladen.
   _____ b. Sie hat jetzt einen neuen Laptop.

6. _____ a. Er braucht sie, um den Fernseher anzumachen.
   _____ b. Lisa will seine laute Musik nicht hören.

7. _____ a. Die Handybatterie ist immer leer.
   _____ b. Das Telefon klingelt.

    Kapitel 4 Lab Activities   **89**

Lab Manual

AUSSPRACHE UND RECHTSCHREIBUNG

The German *l*

To pronounce the German **l**, place your tongue firmly against the ridge behind your top front teeth and open your mouth wider than you would for the English *l*.

lang	Laptop	Telefon	normal	stellen

Unlike the English *l*, the German **l** is always produced with the tongue in the same position no matter what sound comes before or after it. Practice saying **l** after the following consonants or consonant clusters.

Platten	schlafen	Kleid	pflegen	fleißig

Practice saying **l** at the end of words or before the consonants **d, m,** and **n**. Be sure to use the German **l**, even in words that are spelled the same in English and German.

Ball	Spiel	Wald	Film	Zwiebeln

Practice saying the German **l** in front of the consonant clusters **sch** and **ch**.

solch	falsch	Milch	Kölsch	Elch

1 Aussprechen Wiederholen Sie die Wörter, die Sie hören.

1. Lenkrad
2. Fahrplan
3. Öl
4. Klasse
5. schlank
6. Geld
7. Köln
8. welch

2 Nachsprechen Wiederholen Sie die Sätze, die Sie hören.

1. Viele warten an der Bushaltestelle auf den letzten Bus nach Ludwigsfelde.
2. Luise, kannst du das Nummernschild von dem LKW lesen?
3. Lothar hatte leider einen Platten auf einer verlassenen Landstraße.
4. Man soll den Ölstand im Auto regelmäßig kontrollieren.
5. Natürlich hat der Laptop einen DVD-Player und eine Digitalkamera.
6. Klicken Sie auf das Bild, um den Film herunterzuladen.

3 Sprichwörter Wiederholen Sie die Sprichwörter, die Sie hören.

1. Wer im Glashaus sitzt, sollte nicht mit Steinen werfen.
2. Ein Unglück kommt selten allein.

4 Diktat You will hear six sentences. Each will be read twice. Listen carefully and write what you hear.

1. _____
2. _____
3. _____
4. _____
5. _____
6. _____

4B.1 The genitive case

1 **Was hören Sie?** Indicate the word or phrase you hear in each sentence.

1. des Restaurants / das Restaurant
2. die Computerprogramme / der Computerprogramme
3. in die Stadt / der Stadt
4. seinem Neffen / seines Neffen
5. Martinas / Martina

6. Thomas' / Thomas
7. einem Handy / eines Handys
8. der Computer / des Computers
9. einer Computerdatei / eine Computerdatei
10. lauter Bands / lauten Bands

2 **Antworten** You will hear a question about each picture. Answer each question using the genitive form of the words provided. Repeat the correct response after the speaker.

1. der langweilige Lehrer

2. ihr glücklicher Vater

3. ein schlechter Mechaniker

4. die neue Chemielehrerin

5. der kleine Junge

6. Meline

3 **Was fehlt?** You will hear six statements. Complete each sentence using the prepositional phrase you hear after each statement.

Beispiel

You hear: Es regnet, aber Martin und Susanne gehen spazieren. (trotz)
You write: Martin und Susanne gehen ___*trotz des Regens*___ spazieren.

1. Moritz läuft den Marathon _____.

2. Margareta findet ihren Hund _____.

3. Herr Weber arbeitet an seinem Laptop _____.

4. _____ kann Gabriele nichts hören.

5. Rita nimmt den Bus _____.

6. Ich trage die Regenjacke _____.

Lab Manual

4B.2 Demonstratives

1 **Was hören Sie?** Listen to the statements and identify the noun that each demonstrative refers to.

> **Beispiel**
> *You hear:* Wir suchen Kunstbücher. Die brauchen wir für unsere Diplomarbeit.
> *You see:* die Kunstbücher / die Diplomarbeit
> *You mark: die Kunstbücher* _____

1. der blaue Ball / der rote Ball
2. die Bäckerei / die Brötchen
3. der kurze Mantel / der Wollmantel
4. der Lehrer / die Eins
5. Wolfgang Puck / das Essen
6. das Haus / die Möbel
7. der Müll / die Blumenvase
8. Leute / Partys

2 **Was ist richtig?** Based on the statement you hear, choose the appropriate demonstrative pronoun to complete each sentence.

> **Beispiel**
> *You hear:* Wir suchen einen jungen, netten Hund.
> *You see:* Wir möchten (das / den / die) hier adoptieren, bitte.
> *You mark: den* _____

1. (Der / Den / Dem) gefällt das.
2. (Das / Dessen / Die) müssen wir reparieren.
3. (Denen / Deren / Dem) können wir helfen.
4. (Das / Der / Die) hören wir beim Sport an.
5. (Des / Dessen / Deren) Batterie muss geladen werden.
6. (Den / Die / Das) putzt sie heute.

3 **Antworten** Answer the questions using the words provided. Use the appropriate case endings for demonstratives and adjectives. Repeat the correct response after the speaker.

> **Beispiel**
> *You hear:* Welcher Laptop ist kaputt?
> *You see:* dies- / alt-
> *You say: Dieser alte Laptop ist kaputt.*

1. jed- / Schokoladentorte
2. ja / solch- / schwarz-
3. dies- / heiß-
4. manch- / arm-
5. manch- / historisch-
6. dies- / müde-

Lektion 1A, Folge 1   Fotoroman

Frohes neues Jahr!

1   **Was passt?** Match the first part of each sentence with the correct ending.

_____ 1. Torsten möchte an Silvester...   a. gesehen.

_____ 2. Meline und Lorenzo wollen...   b. gekommen.

_____ 3. George und Hans haben Licht...   c. eingeladen.

_____ 4. Sie sind von einer Party in Kreuzberg...   d. lernen.

_____ 5. Hans' Eltern haben George zu Ostern...   e. gebacken.

_____ 6. Hans hat einen Stollen...   f. essen gehen.

2   **Antworten Sie** Answer the questions in complete sentences.

1. Warum ist Sabite traurig?

_____

_____

2. Welche Pläne haben Meline und Lorenzo?

_____

_____

3. Warum will Sabite nicht zum Brandenburger Tor gehen?

_____

_____

4. Warum kommen Hans und George in die Wohnung von Meline und Sabite?

_____

_____

5. Was bringen sie mit?

_____

_____

3   **Sie sind dran** Write a description of a birthday party you attended. Who was invited? What foods were served? What did people wear? What gifts were given?

_____

_____

_____

_____

_____

_____

_____

_____

_____

     Kapitel 1 Fotoroman Activities   **93**

Video Manual

Lektion 1B, Folge 2   **Fotoroman**

Sehr attraktiv, George!

1   **Sortieren Sie**   Number the events in the order in which they occur.

_____ a. George probiert neue Kleidung an.

_____ b. Meline findet eine schöne Handtasche.

_____ c. George sieht ein hübsches Mädchen.

_____ d. George und Meline gehen zur Kaiser-Wilhelm-Gedächtnis-Kirche.

_____ e. Meline trifft Esteban Aurelio Gómez de la Garza.

2   **Wer ist das?**   Select the person each statement describes.

1. Er ist unhöflich zu Meline gewesen.
   a. Torsten   b. George   c. Lorenzo

2. Er ist den Skulpturenboulevard entlang spaziert.
   a. George   b. Hans   c. Lorenzo

3. Er weiß viel über Architektur.
   a. Torsten   b. Lukas   c. George

4. Er studiert VWL in Österreich.
   a. George   b. Torsten   c. Lukas

5. Er arbeitet im Bereich internationale Finanzen.
   a. Lorenzo   b. Torsten   c. Lukas

6. Er studiert Geschichte.
   a. Torsten   b. Hans   c. Lukas

3   **Sie sind dran**   Imagine that you are invited to a costume party. Describe what you are wearing to the party.

_____

_____

_____

_____

_____

_____

_____

_____

_____

_____

_____

_____

_____

Video Manual

Lektion 2A, Folge 3   Fotoroman

Besuch von Max

---

1   **Richtig oder falsch?** Indicate whether each statement is **richtig** or **falsch**.

	richtig	falsch
1. Max bleibt übers Wochenende in Berlin.	○	○
2. Bis Sonntagabend muss er wieder in Straubing sein.	○	○
3. George muss noch Mathematik lernen.	○	○
4. Die Lampen und Vorhänge in der Wohnung gehören Meline.	○	○
5. Am Weihnachtsmorgen ging George in die Garage.	○	○
6. Er überraschte Opa Otto mit der Weihnachtsgans.	○	○
7. Er rannte schnell aus der Küche.	○	○
8. Die ganze Familie kennt das Rezept für die Weihnachtsgans.	○	○

---

2   **Erklären Sie** After Max meets Meline, there seems to be some tension between the two brothers. Describe what Hans and Max are each feeling in this scene, and why.

_____
_____
_____
_____
_____
_____
_____
_____

---

3   **Sie sind dran** Imagine you are going to spend a year in Germany. What city would you like to live in? Describe where you will live and what you want your apartment or house to be like.

_____
_____
_____
_____
_____
_____
_____
_____
_____
_____

Video Manual

     Kapitel 2 Fotoroman Activities

Lektion 2B, Folge 4   **Fotoroman**

Ich putze gern

1 **Sortieren Sie** Number the events in the order in which they occur.

_____ a. George hilft Meline bei der Hausarbeit.

_____ b. Meline telefoniert mit ihrer Freundin Beatrice.

_____ c. Meline muss die Wäsche bügeln.

_____ d. Sabite und Meline wollen die Wohnung aufräumen.

_____ e. Meline geht zum Tee zur Großmutter von Beatrice.

2 **Korrigieren Sie** Each statement below contains one piece of false information. Underline the incorrect word(s), and write the correct word(s) in the space provided.

1. Meline trifft ihre Schwester Beatrice in einer halben Stunde. _____

2. Beatrice besucht ihre Mutter in Wilmersdorf. _____

3. Sabite muss den Abfall rausbringen. _____

4. George hatte als Kind ein Zimmer mit seiner Halbschwester. _____

5. Georg hilft Meline bei der Hausarbeit. _____

6. Meline möchte am Abend einen Rock anziehen. _____

3 **Sie sind dran** Imagine that you are dividing household chores with your roommate. Write a conversation in which you discuss which chores you will each do. Mention at least six tasks.

_____

_____

_____

_____

_____

_____

_____

_____

_____

_____

_____

_____

_____

_____

_____

_____

_____

Video Manual

Lektion 3A, Folge 5 — Fotoroman

Berlin von oben

1 **Was passt?** Match the first part of these sentences with the correct endings.

_____ 1. Der Lake Michigan...
_____ 2. Der Frühling ist Georges...
_____ 3. George probiert...
_____ 4. George ist in den USA...
_____ 5. Der Fernsehturm ist das...
_____ 6. George hat...

a. nicht mit Frauen befreundet.
b. viele Architekturbilder gesehen.
c. beeinflusst das Klima in Milwaukee.
d. höchste Gebäude in Deutschland.
e. Lieblingsjahreszeit.
f. einen neuen Kleidungsstil aus.

2 **Antworten Sie** Answer these questions in complete sentences.

1. Warum ist der Frühling Georges Lieblingsjahreszeit?

2. Warum probiert George neue Kleidung an?

3. Wobei hat George Sabite geholfen?

4. Worauf kann man vom Dach des Hotels sehen?

5. Warum war Torsten überrascht?

3 **Sie sind dran** What is your favorite season? Give reasons for your answer.

Kapitel 3 Fotoroman Activities **97**

Video Manual

Lektion 3B, Folge 6   Fotoroman

Ein Sommer in der Türkei?

1 **Richtig oder falsch?** Indicate whether each statement is **richtig** or **falsch**.

		richtig	falsch
1.	Familie Yilmaz will den Sommer in der Türkei verbringen.	○	○
2.	Sabite und Zeynep waren seit drei Jahren nicht mehr im Ausland.	○	○
3.	Sie wollen in der Türkei etwas über Architektur erfahren.	○	○
4.	Zeynep möchte Zimmerservice bestellen.	○	○
5.	Am Flughafen möchte sie die Passagiere fotografieren.	○	○
6.	Anke glaubt, dass es bei Problemen zwischen Partnern nie nur um eine Sache geht.	○	○
7.	Sabite glaubt, dass Torsten ihre Kunst nicht verstehen möchte.	○	○
8.	Meline versteht Sabites Kunst.	○	○

2 **Erklären Sie** Do you think Sabite's relationship with Torsten could be improved? Explain your answer.

_____

_____

_____

_____

_____

_____

_____

_____

3 **Sie sind dran** List four places where you would like to go on vacation. Then list two activities you might do in each place. Do not list the same activity more than once.

Ziel	Aktivität 1	Aktivität 2
1. _____	_____	_____
2. _____	_____	_____
3. _____	_____	_____
4. _____	_____	_____
5. _____	_____	_____

Lektion 4A, Folge 7   Fotoroman

Ein Ende mit Schrecken

1   **Richtig oder falsch?** Indicate whether each statement is **richtig** or **falsch**.

	richtig	falsch
1. Milwaukee hat ein sehr gutes S-Bahn-System.	○	○
2. George fährt mit seinem Auto zur Uni und zurück.	○	○
3. Auf deutschen Autobahnen gibt es keine Geschwindigkeitsbegrenzung.	○	○
4. Georges Mutter fährt gern sehr schnell.	○	○
5. Sabite hat im Restaurant mit Lorenzo über Architektur gesprochen.	○	○
6. Torsten hat Silvester mit Sabite gefeiert.	○	○
7. Sabite findet George, Hans und Meline lustiger als Torsten.	○	○
8. Nachdem sie mit Sabite telefoniert hatten, haben George und Hans die U-Bahn genommen.	○	○

2   **Erklären Sie** Why did Sabite and Torsten break up? Describe at least three things Sabite and Torsten said or did that led to the end of their relationship.

_____
_____
_____
_____
_____
_____
_____

3   **Sie sind dran** Describe a time when you had car trouble, or other problems with transportation. What happened? What did you do?

_____
_____
_____
_____
_____
_____
_____
_____

Video Manual

Lektion 4B, Folge 8   Fotoroman

Ein Spaziergang durch Spandau

1 | **Sortieren Sie** Number the events in the order in which they occur.

_____ a. Meline entschuldigt sich bei Hans im Café.

_____ b. George und Sabite treffen ein älteres Paar.

_____ c. George und Sabite besuchen die Zitadelle in Spandau.

_____ d. Hans steht auf und lässt Meline im Café sitzen.

_____ e. Hans klopft an die Tür von Melines Wohnung.

2 | **Korrigieren Sie** Each statement below contains one piece of false information. Underline the incorrect word(s), and write the correct word(s) in the space provided.

1. Die Spandauer Zitadelle wurde im 18. Jahrhundert erbaut. _____

2. Die Zitadelle ist das größte Bauwerk in Berlin. _____

3. Sabite hat Torstens Krawatte behalten. _____

4. Meline gibt Hans etwas Geld und eine Jacke. _____

5. Meline schreibt George, dass sie Hans ins Kino geschickt hat. _____

6. Der alte Mann sagt, Berlin ist ein herrlicher Ort, um verheiratet zu sein. _____

7. Die alte Frau sagt, dass Georges Augen leuchten, wenn Sabite redet. _____

8. Meline hat während eines Chats eine Datei gedruckt. _____

3 | **Sie sind dran** Name three technological devices or services and write a sentence explaining how you use each one.

1. _____

_____

_____

2. _____

_____

_____

3. _____

_____

_____

Video Manual